The Campus History Series

WESTERN COLLEGE FOR WOMEN

KUMLER MEMORIAL CHAPEL. Sisters Anna Kumler Wight (Western class of 1879) and Ella Kumler McKelvy commissioned the chapel to memorialize their parents, the Reverend Jeremiah "Jerry" Prophet Elias Kumler and Abigail "Abbie" Goulding Kumler, and their grandfather Elias Kumler, an early benefactor and longtime trustee of the seminary. Jerry was a student at Miami and Abbie a teacher at Western when they met. A small church in Normandy provided the inspiration for the Norman Gothic design. After the dedication of Kumler Chapel in 1918, church services were moved here from the Peabody Hall chapel. The heart of the campus, Kumler Chapel became the choice location for special events, including commencements, concerts, lectures, and of course, weddings. (Photograph by Jeff Sabo, Miami University.)

ON THE COVER: Led by Helen Peabody, principal, the students and faculty of Western Female Seminary are gathered here on the porch and steps of Seminary Hall for a formal group photograph in 1879. Faculty and students would continue to make this a tradition of college life for years to come. (Courtesy of Western College Memorial Archives.)

ON THE BACK COVER: Students, faculty, staff, and guests at Western enjoy a leisurely day on the lawn in front of the renovated Peabody Hall around 1889, approximately 18 years after fire had destroyed the building. Later renovations included electric lights, installed in 1889, and student rooms on the first and second floors, added in the summer of 1890. (Courtesy of Western College Memorial Archives.)

The Campus History Series

WESTERN COLLEGE FOR WOMEN

JACQUELINE JOHNSON

ARCADIA PUBLISHING

ISBN 978-1-4671-1058-7

Published by Arcadia Publishing
Charleston, South Carolina

Printed in the United States of America

Library of Congress Catalog Card Number: 2013951200

For all general information, please contact Arcadia Publishing:
Telephone 843-853-2070
Fax 843-853-0044
E-mail sales@arcadiapublishing.com
For customer service and orders:
Toll-Free 1-888-313-2665

Visit us on the Internet at www.arcadiapublishing.com

CONTENTS

FOREWORD

A Western alumna once said it was a place "to prepare to go out into the world and do good." From its beginning in 1855 until its merger with Miami University in 1974, the Western College in Oxford, Ohio, had a distinctly communal character. "Most colleges have residences," Dean Phyllis Hoyt wrote, "but that does not make them residential colleges. . . It means that living together and learning together are compatible, that they support and reinforce each other. They make exchanging ideas and learning from each other a vital part of the total experience, in many ways the most important aspect of the college years."

Jacqueline Johnson regards this book as a visual, social history that evokes Western's changing residential character. Readers of academic histories and memoirs should be able to see here images revealing the daily lives of students for more than a century. Those familiar with institutions for women know they have produced graduates with a lifelong passion for their college. These pages suggest how that bond has been created and document the rich life of a remarkable and fondly remembered institution.

—Curtis W. Ellison
Oxford, Ohio

ACKNOWLEDGMENTS

When I began as the archivist of Western College Memorial Archives, I was intrigued by the available materials and quickly discovered that I had had a similar educational journey. Like my beloved Limestone College, Western College was established in the mid-19th century as a religious female institution in a small town, and both would become highly respected coeducational colleges. Thanks to my colleagues at the Western College Alumnae Association—Mackenzie Becker Rice, Debbie Baker, Judy Waldron, and Kaye Wolke—for their encouragement and support to depict the historical experience of Western College. Thanks to the Western College Alumnae Association Board of Trustees. Special thanks to Catherine Cooper for her advice, guidance, and editorial skills. Curtis Ellison, who served as my local history expert, was truly a blessing. Thanks to Valerie Elliott, local history librarian, as well as Renea Frey for the first round of proofing and editing. Thanks to my colleagues in the university archives, Bob Schmidt and Lynn Bartram Smith. The journey has been easier with these friends who have taught me how to "persevere." Thanks to the following Western alumnae, faculty, staff, volunteers, and friends for sharing their stories and research with me: Donavon Auble, Priscilla Berry, Helene Cella, Debbie Davidson, Elizabeth Gerber, Rita Greene, Elizabeth Johnson, Debbie Keebler, Mary Lee Keebler, Susan Lantz, Barbara Mecklenborg, Susan Rasman, Cindy Rothermel, Eleanore Vail, and Jocelyn Woodson-Reed. Their help has greatly enabled this book to create a pictorial and historical story of Western College.

I also thank my colleagues at Miami University: Elizabeth Brice, Jerome Conley, Lori Chapin, Suzanne Haag, Helen Sheumaker, Marilyn Elzey, Manal Osman, Kwabena Sekyere, Laura Sheppard, Elias Tzoc, and Barry Zaslow. Thanks also to Mary Margaret Schley, my faithful editor, who guided me throughout the process. Your e-mails and phone calls kept me on track.

Unless otherwise noted, images appear courtesy of Western College Memorial Archives.

Finally, I give all honor and praise to God, who has guided me throughout this project. "Trust in the Lord with all thine heart and lean not upon your own understanding. In all your ways acknowledge him and he shall direct your paths." (Proverbs 3:5–6.) I am always grateful for the opportunities He has brought to my life.

—Jacqueline Johnson
Archivist, Western College Memorial Archives

INTRODUCTION

Considering it his God-given duty to establish a school to "check the frivolity and wrecklessness of our young ladies," the Reverend Daniel Tenney, pastor of the Second Presbyterian Church in Oxford, Ohio, set his resolve and—together with his equally dedicated wife, Mary—went about the business of gathering sponsors. Miraculously, the Tenneys raised $25,000 in the month of June, and on July 14, 1853, Western Female Seminary was born.

Western College holds a prominent place in the history of women's education and education in general in Oxford, which was established as a college town in 1810, one year after Miami University was chartered. During the 1850s, the town was the home of four other institutions of higher learning: Oxford Theological Seminary (1838) and three women's schools, Oxford Female Institute (1849), Western Female Seminary (1853), and Oxford Female College (1854). By 1928, only Miami and Western College for Women remained.

Located on what was then Oxford's eastern border, this "daughter of Mount Holyoke" sought to provide women with the same access as men to an education both wholesome and worthwhile. In 1837, in South Hadley, Massachusetts, Mary Lyon founded Mount Holyoke Female Seminary, which quickly gained national recognition for its rigorous academic discipline and religious training. Inspired by Mount Holyoke, the Tenneys, who had come to Oxford from New Hampshire, where they were familiar with the teaching philosophy of Mary Lyon, were determined to establish a similar institution dedicated to what was later known as the "Holyoke plan."

With encouragement from leaders of Oxford's Second Presbyterian Church, a board of trustees was organized, James Fisher of Oxford donated the land for the school (originally, his potato patch), and in September 1855, the school opened. As the "western" embodiment of Mount Holyoke, the institution offered low-cost, high-quality education made possible by another element of the Holyoke plan, the "domestic system." In addition to their studies, the "young ladies" performed all the domestic work of the seminary. Many were inspired by their religious education to undertake careers in mission work and traveled to distant countries in Asia and the Middle East—and to the "Wild West" of their home country. In fact, a young woman of American Indian and French descent from the Dakota Territory became Western's first "foreign student."

The Western board of trustees selected Helen Peabody, a 29-year-old Mount Holyoke alumna, to be the first principal of the Western Female Seminary. A devoted student and dear friend of Mary Lyon's (she taught at her alma mater for five years after graduating in 1848), Miss Peabody used her teaching experience at Mount Holyoke and her views on women's intellectual pursuits to set the tone for the new school.

The seminary opened its doors in 1855 with 10 faculty members, all from Mount Holyoke, and 52 students. The majority came from Ohio, Illinois, Missouri, Pennsylvania, Indiana, and Kentucky. Miss Peabody served as the principal architect of the Western curriculum from 1855 to 1888. Students studied astronomy, geology, biology, physiology, botany, physics, and chemistry. Plane geometry and trigonometry were required, as were Greek, French, Latin, English, and history. Helen Peabody's faith, energy, foresight, and perseverance helped Western survive the Civil War and major fires at Seminary Hall (the main and, until 1892, only building) in 1860 and 1871. She exhorted "her girls" to be "masters of the situation anywhere," a mantra used over and over again for generations to come. But in 1864, an outbreak of typhus resulted in several deaths and forced the school to close for the remainder of that academic year; the seminary was able to reopen the following fall. Over the course of its history, the Western curriculum moved from a seminary model to a liberal arts program with an international emphasis and, near the end of its history, an individualized studies approach.

In 1888, Miss Peabody retired, and the board of trustees elected the seminary's second principal, Leila S. McKee, an alumna of both the Western Female Seminary and Wellesley College. The visionary and vivacious Leila McKee had attracted their attention a few years earlier with a speech in which she laid out her ideas for a new direction in women's education. Indeed, it was the right time, and she was the right person to incorporate gradual changes in the curriculum that would move Western forward, on a par with women's colleges in the East. She also brought with her a love of pageants and picnics and began such traditions as Tree Day, which was celebrated until the college closed. In 1894, Western became The Western: A College and Seminary for Women, with course work leading to a bachelor of arts degree. In 1904, the word "Seminary" was dropped, Western became the Western College for Women, and Miss McKee became its first president. The college was subsequently led by nine more presidents and experienced a relatively long period of financial stability and academic success.

In 1910, noted composer Edgar Stillman Kelley came to Western as the first artist-in-residence at an American college. William Waddell Boyd, president from 1914 to 1931, was responsible for shaping the 20th-century campus. Patterson Place became the home of the president. Ernst Nature Theatre, a new outdoor amphitheater, was dedicated, and four buildings were constructed: Kumler Memorial Chapel, Presser Hall, Mary Lyon Hall, and the lodge. Stone bridges to facilitate traversing the rolling campus, and which so enhance its charm, were also built. During the United States' involvement in World War I, students called "Farmerettes" joined the war effort by planting and harvesting crops and canning food. In 1942, a similar effort was made with Victory Gardens.

With the arrival of Pres. Herrick B. Young in 1954, international students and faculty were actively recruited, international seminars were instituted, a global emphasis was added to the curriculum, and Western became a leader in intercultural studies. *Time* magazine published a full-page advertisement with the headline "Western College: Who in the World Goes There?" In 1964, the administration of Western College allowed the campus to be used for training sessions for volunteers participating in the Mississippi Summer Project. Later known as "Freedom Summer," it gained national attention, assuring Western College's place in the history of the American civil rights movement. In 1971, Western instituted the innovative program "Freedom With Responsibility," which permitted students to design their own curriculum in consultation with tutors and professors.

Western College remained a women's residential college until 1972, when it became coeducational. Faced with growing financial difficulties exacerbated by a national recession, Western College closed and the campus was merged with neighboring Miami University in 1974. Today, Western alumnae/i, following in their predecessors' footsteps, remain loyal daughters and sons linked to their alma mater through a thriving alumnae association and are active and influential members of their communities worldwide.

One

Daughter of Mount Holyyoke

Opening the Gate (1855–1888)

Helen Peabody. Helen Peabody served as the first principal of Western, from 1855 to 1888. Summoned to establish a "Mount Holyoke in the West," she selected faculty, created curriculum, and led the seminary through two major fires and the Civil War. After 33 years at Western, she retired in 1888 and moved to Pasadena, California. Unable to return to campus for the June 1905 Golden Jubilee celebration, she received a telegram announcing that Seminary Hall was to be renamed Helen Peabody Hall in her honor. She died in October of that year.

Daniel and Mary Tenney. By working to found the Western Female Seminary, these Massachusetts natives achieved their long-held dream to support education for women in "the West." A pastor at Oxford's Second Presbyterian Church, Daniel Tenney organized Western's board of trustees, drew up a charter, solicited building funds, and requested that Mount Holyoke recommend someone "fitted by education and temperament" to serve as Western's principal.

Miss Peabody. An 1848 Mount Holyoke graduate and student of Mary Lyon, young Helen Peabody was called to lead the new seminary. With heavy heart—for she had to leave St. Louis, where she was caring for her widowed brother's infant son—but never hesitating to accept the challenge, she came to Oxford ready to do God's will. (Photograph by Toepfert, Cincinnati, Ohio.)

"DEDICATION HYMN." Written by the Reverend Thomas Spencer, this hymn was performed for the first time at the seminary dedication on September 20, 1855, and performed thereafter on special occasions. Though the original melody is unknown, in May 1954, Ruth Bracher, professor of music, set it to music to commemorate the Western College Centennial.

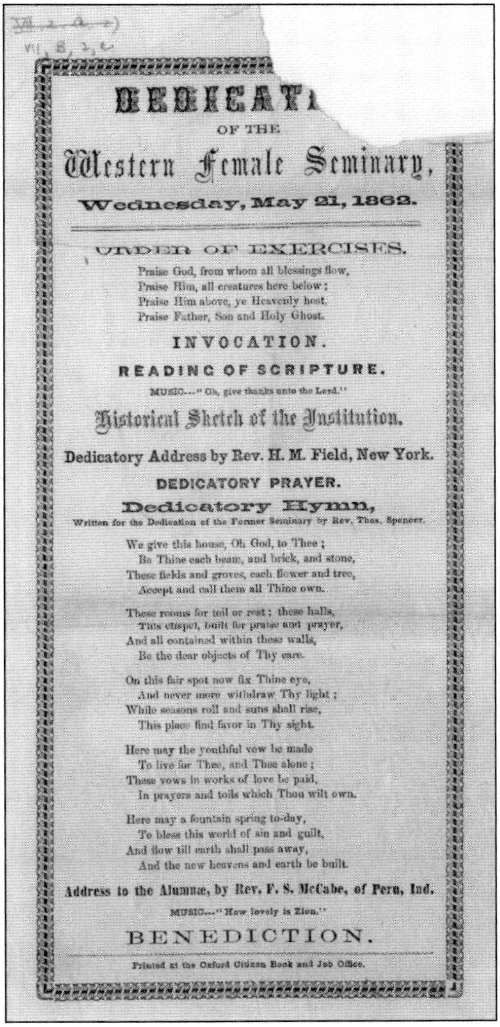
DEDICATI[ON]
OF THE
Western Female Seminary,
Wednesday, May 21, 1862.

ORDER OF EXERCISES.

Praise God, from whom all blessings flow,
Praise Him, all creatures here below;
Praise Him above, ye Heavenly host,
Praise Father, Son and Holy Ghost.

INVOCATION.

READING OF SCRIPTURE.

MUSIC—"Oh, give thanks unto the Lord."

Historical Sketch of the Institution.

Dedicatory Address by Rev. H. M. Field, New York.

DEDICATORY PRAYER.

Dedicatory Hymn,

Written for the Dedication of the Former Seminary by Rev. Thos. Spencer.

We give this house, Oh God, to Thee;
Be Thine each beam, and brick, and stone,
These fields and groves, each flower and tree,
Accept and call them all Thine own.

These rooms for toil or rest; these halls,
This chapel, built for praise and prayer,
And all contained within these walls,
Be the dear objects of Thy care.

On this fair spot now fix Thine eye,
And never more withdraw Thy light;
While seasons roll and suns shall rise,
This place find favor in Thy sight.

Here may the youthful vow be made
To live for Thee, and Thee alone;
These vows in works of love be paid,
In prayers and toils which Thou wilt own.

Here may a fountain spring to-day,
To bless this world of sin and guilt,
And flow till earth shall pass away,
And the new heavens and earth be built.

Address to the Alumnæ, by Rev. F. S. McCabe, of Peru, Ind.

MUSIC—"How lovely is Zion."

BENEDICTION.

Printed at the Oxford Citizen Book and Job Office.

"HOW FIRM A FOUNDATION." This hymn was sung for chapel services, processionals, and major campus events and became the official seminary hymn in 1856. As a reminder of their religious faith and of the strength of solidarity, pupils sang this song the morning of January 14, 1860, while sheltering at Oxford Female College after the first seminary fire and again after the second fire in 1871.

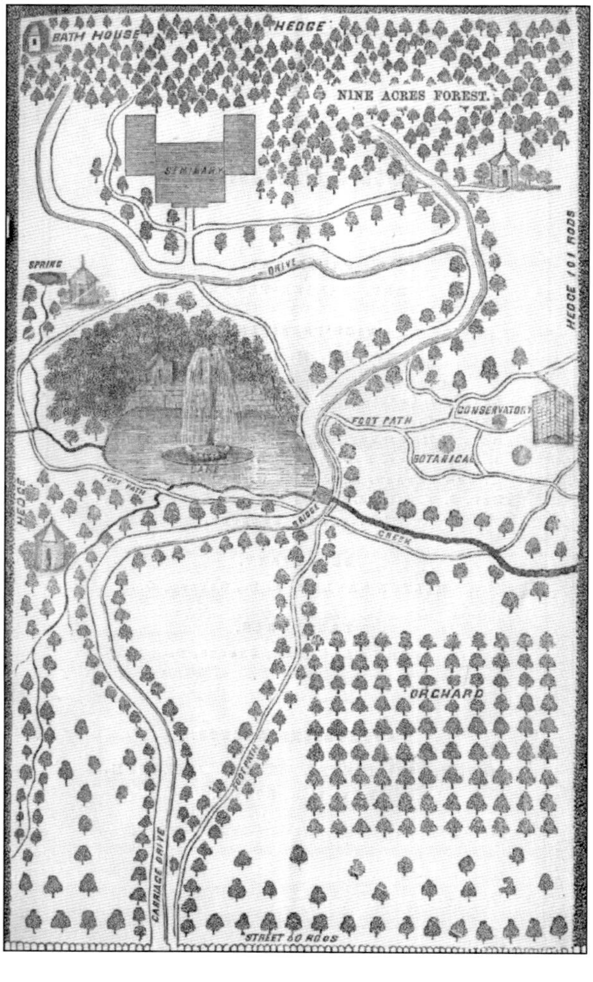

Campus Grounds. Pictured here in 1877, the rolling hills, ponds, and forests of the original 30-acre campus provided a backdrop for the rigorous curriculum students pursued. Today, Oxford, Ohio, would not be considered "the West," yet at the time Western Female Seminary was founded, many regarded this region as a relatively isolated western frontier of the "civilized" eastern part of the United States.

Seminary Grounds. This illustration from the 1894 edition of the *Western Circular* shows structures, paths, roads, water resources, and orchards on campus. The circular was published for friends and patrons and describes the seminary's educational departments, Christian beliefs, academic requirements, conditions of admission, age requirements, tuition, and courses of study, such as botany, rhetoric, chemistry, astronomy, physiology, and logic.

ENGINE HOUSE. The Engine House, pictured about 1877, was constructed shortly after the second Seminary Hall was built in 1861. Its purpose was to provide heat and, later, electricity to the college. Though it has been modernized, it is still in use. This photograph was taken by Henry Peabody, brother of Susan Peabody and nephew of Helen Peabody. He was a noted photographer who specialized in marine, landscape, and architectural photography.

SEMINARY HALL FIRE, 1860. Established in 1853, the Western Female Seminary was housed in this building with classrooms, a chapel, administrative offices, and dormitory rooms. Until 1892, it remained the only building on the rolling, wooded, 30-acre farmland east of Oxford, Ohio. During the first two decades, Western was severely tested as its Seminary Hall was twice ravaged by fire. The first fire, caused by a defective flue, began on January 14, 1860, in the early morning hours. As rain turned to sleet, Miss Peabody stood in front of the burning building and called the roll until everyone answered, then offered a prayer "for our deliverance."

Seminary Hall Fire, 1871. A second Seminary Hall, rebuilt in 1861, caught fire 10 years later, on April 7, 1871. At 1:00 a.m., smoke and flames from an overheated oven in the kitchen poured through the registers. This fire made more rapid progress than the 1860 fire, but destroyed less. Walls were standing the next day, with only a portion of them partly in ruins. A third structure using the same walls was erected and stands today as Peabody Hall on the Western campus.

CIRCULAR

OF THE

WESTERN

Female Seminary,

OXFORD, OHIO.

SECOND EDITION.

CINCINNATI:

BEN FRANKLIN MAMMOTH STEAM PRINTING HOUSE, WALNUT STREET,

1854.

CIRCULAR, **1856.** This 12-page catalog was designed to attract students. It included a statement of Christian philosophy, course descriptions, admission requirements, tuition, accommodations, and a schedule of classes. It listed trustees, faculty, and 152 enrolled students. Board and tuition cost $60 a year for daughters of clergy and for daughters of $100 donors. Others paid $2.50 per week. No one under 15 years of age was admitted. A catalog was published each year, expanding to reflect Western's growing population and educational offerings.

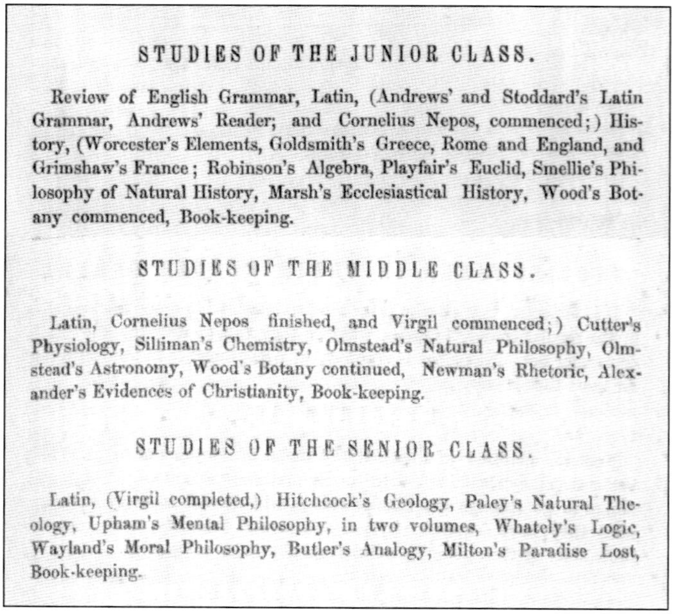

STUDIES OF THE JUNIOR CLASS.

Review of English Grammar, Latin, (Andrews' and Stoddard's Latin Grammar, Andrews' Reader; and Cornelius Nepos, commenced;) History, (Worcester's Elements, Goldsmith's Greece, Rome and England, and Grimshaw's France; Robinson's Algebra, Playfair's Euclid, Smellie's Philosophy of Natural History, Marsh's Ecclesiastical History, Wood's Botany commenced, Book-keeping.

STUDIES OF THE MIDDLE CLASS.

Latin, Cornelius Nepos finished, and Virgil commenced;) Cutter's Physiology, Silliman's Chemistry, Olmstead's Natural Philosophy, Olmstead's Astronomy, Wood's Botany continued, Newman's Rhetoric, Alexander's Evidences of Christianity, Book-keeping.

STUDIES OF THE SENIOR CLASS.

Latin, (Virgil completed,) Hitchcock's Geology, Paley's Natural Theology, Upham's Mental Philosophy, in two volumes, Whately's Logic, Wayland's Moral Philosophy, Butler's Analogy, Milton's Paradise Lost, Book-keeping.

CURRICULUM, 1856. To be admitted, prospective students were required to have a good knowledge of several fields, including mental arithmetic and US history, as well as acquaintance with theologian and logician Isaac Watts's *Improvement of the Mind*. Using standard textbooks of the day, courses of study included Latin, natural philosophy, ancient and modern history, rhetoric, and bookkeeping. In 1866, the seminary made Bible courses available to students.

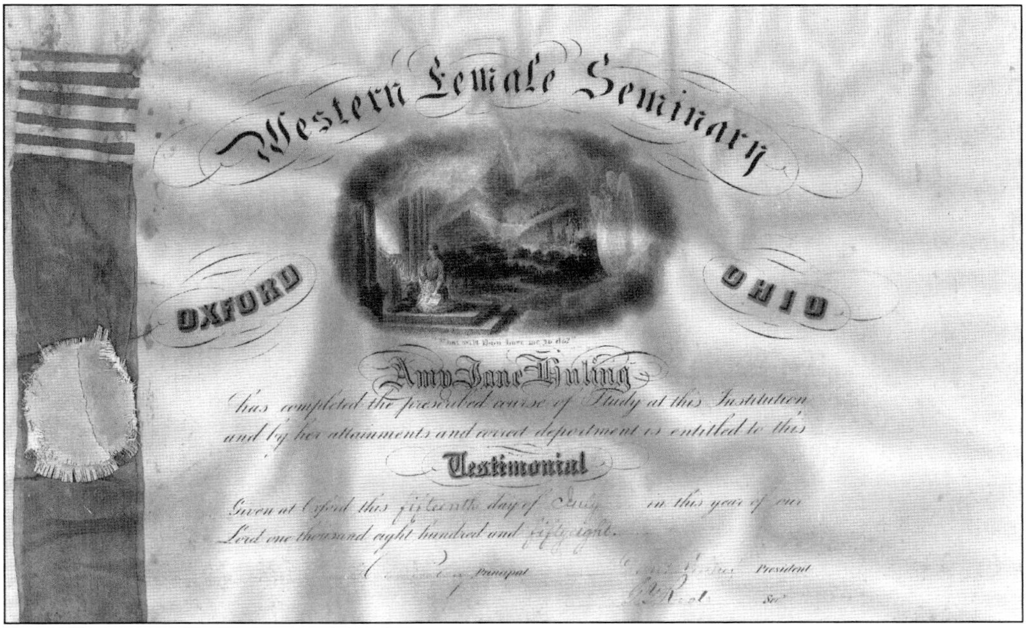

HULING DIPLOMA. From Bantam, Ohio, Amy Jane Huling was one of 23 students in the first class to complete the three-year seminary degree course in 1858. The ribbon is affixed with the original seminary seal. Studies included Paley's *Natural Theology*, Upham's *Mental Philosophy*, Whately's *Elements of Logic*, Butler's *Analogy of Religion*, Milton's *Paradise Lost*, Latin, and trigonometry.

ELIZABETHTOWN. After the first seminary building burned, all but the senior class and its teachers were sent home. Students in the class of 1860 completed their studies in a vacant house owned by trustee James Fisher—which became fondly known as "Little Western"—and graduated on schedule. In September, the "middle" class of 25 pupils returned to carry on their work in the house pictured here, rented by trustees in Elizabethtown, Ohio, about 30 miles from Oxford.

Domestic Duties. Based upon the domestic system employed at Mount Holyoke, the young women were required to carry out most of their own household duties, including cooking, cleaning, and sewing. They engaged in these activities for an hour or more each day, helping to keep the cost of tuition and board low for their families, yet allowing ample time for academics as well as religious and social activities.

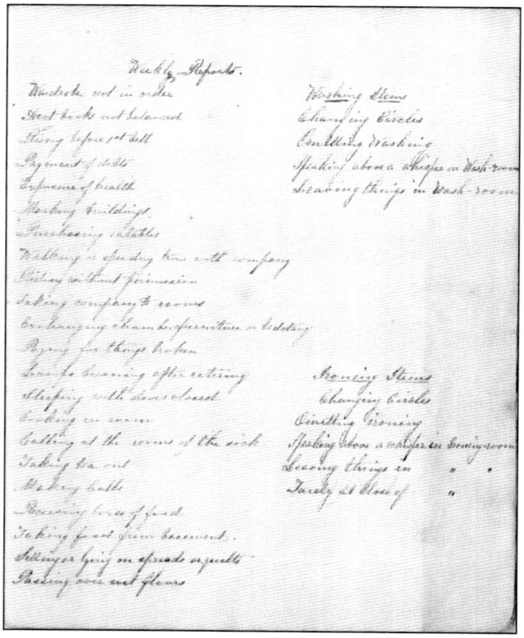

Weekly Reports.

Wardrobe not in order
Account books not balanced
Rising before 1st bell
Payment of debts
Exposure of health
Marking buildings
Purchasing eatables
Walking or spending time with company
Riding without permission
Taking company to rooms
Exchanging chamber furniture or bedding
Paying for things broken
[illegible] after entering
[illegible]
Cooking in room
Calling at the rooms of the sick
Taking tea out
Making calls
Receiving boxes of food
Taking food from basement
Sitting or lying on spreads or quilts
Passing over wet floors

Washing Items
Changing Circles
Omitting Washing
Speaking above a whisper in Wash-room
Leaving things in Wash-room

Ironing Items
Changing Circles
Omitting Ironing
Speaking above a whisper in Ironing-room
Leaving things in " "
Tardy at Close of "

Infractions. The *Western Section Book: 1858–1859* provides detailed rules and regulations that students at Western Female Seminary were expected to obey while enrolled. There was a long list of infractions, such as "Wardrobe not in order," "Rising before first bell," "Riding without permission," "Taking company to rooms," "Sitting or lying on spreads or quilts," and "Delaying in halls." These were tracked for each student on an ongoing basis.

The Green Stool. Alumnae remembered Helen Peabody's "green stool" as the site of reprimands and confessions of "exceptions" to rules. Here, Clara Belle Brown (class of 1875) and another student parody the stern admonitions of Miss Peabody—an occurrence common enough that the ominous expression "going to sit on the green stool" was well known at the "Sem." This octagonal stool, covered in green velvet, was saved from both fires and is preserved in the Patterson Place Museum.

Missionary Work. Many of Western's graduates became missionaries, traveling the world and sending back news of their adventures in places such as Iran, Persia, China, Korea, Mexico, Turkey, Laos, and India. This photograph shows Mary Katherina Hesser with her school students in Kanazawa, Japan, in 1882. To promote and support the missionary work of Western alumnae, a missionary society was formed with Helen Peabody as its first president.

Helen Peabody and the Class of 1866. Everyone was touched in some way by the American Civil War, yet Western remained open and classes were taught. The war brought tragedy to Western in 1864 when a typhus epidemic struck the seminary after soldiers had stopped to visit. The disease caused the deaths of some students and faculty. Western closed that year but reopened the next fall.

Early Faculty. Seated on the seminary porch steps in 1878 are, from left to right, the misses Caroline White, botany and chemistry; Alice W. Milligan, music; Nellie McKinney, painting and drawing; Helen Peabody, principal; Anna Leonard, instrumental music; Bessie Nelson, English; Harriet Day, vocal and instrumental music; Sue Timberman; Sarah Janes; Sarah Skinner, Latin; Emma Paige; Emily Jessup, history and philosophy; and Mary Sheppard, English. (Photograph by Henry G. Peabody.)

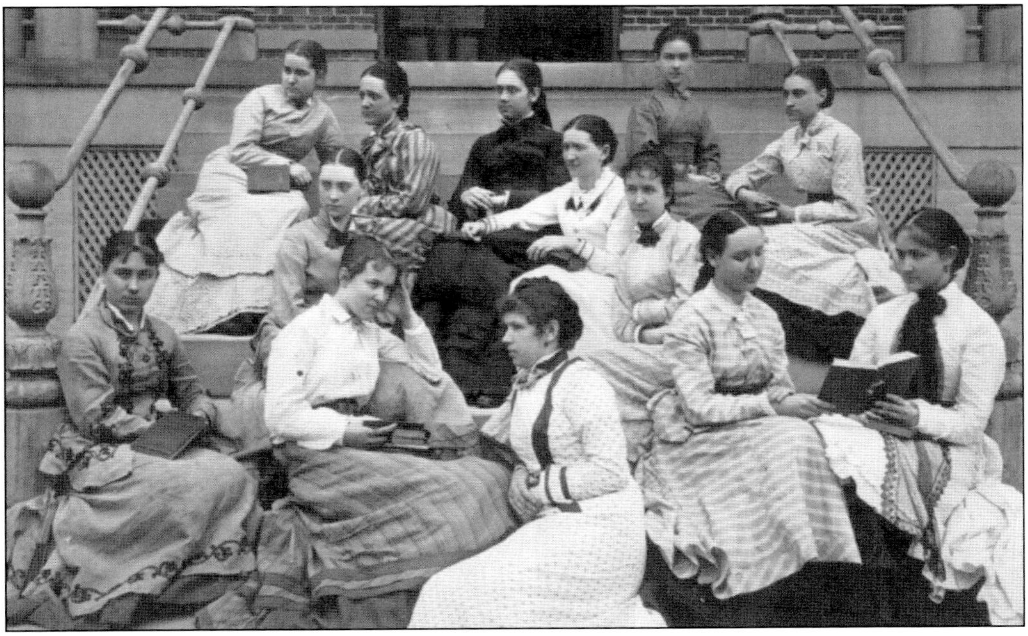

Class of 1877. The graduating class of 1877 included Leila McKee (far right), who became principal and then president of Western—the only alumna to do so. She was from Danville, Kentucky, where her father, John Lapsley McKee, was a professor and vice president at Centre College. She went on to earn degrees from both Wellesley College and Centre College. (Photograph by Henry G. Peabody.)

Susan Wade Peabody. Beloved niece of Helen Peabody, Susan was the daughter of Helen's brother, the Reverend Charles Peabody, and came to live at the seminary after the death of her mother. After graduating from Western in 1882, she earned a bachelor of arts from Wellesley and a doctorate from the University of Chicago but remained ever loyal to her first alma mater. Susan Peabody became a trustee in 1919 and later received an honorary degree from Western College. She is pictured here (at left) with fellow undergraduates. (Photograph by Henry G. Peabody.)

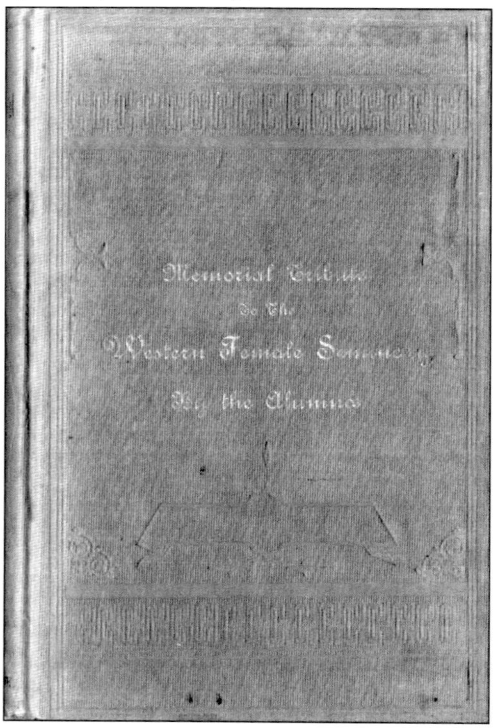

Memorial 25th Anniversary. In 1880, to celebrate the Western Seminary's 25th anniversary, Helen Peabody summoned all alumnae to a homecoming reunion with the words, "Has the anchor held in the storm?" It was the first official meeting of alumnae, and the following year, they published *A Memorial Tribute to the Western Female Seminary*, in which they told the story of the seminary and their experiences. Alumnae continued to be an active force in the development and history of Western.

PERMANENT SCHOLARSHIP.

No. 7

$1,000.

In consideration of One Thousand Dollars, paid to the WESTERN FEMALE SEMINARY, Oxford, Ohio, by Francis M. Foote Esq. the Trustees of said Seminary hereby covenant with Francis M. Foote & his heirs and assigns, forever to EDUCATE in their Institution, without charge for Tuition and Board, one pupil at a time, perpetually. Provided, always, that the candidate possesses the requisite qualifications for admission, and while in the Institution, conforms to its Rules and Regulations.

Provided, also, that the regular charges for Music and for Warming and Lighting the Building, be regularly paid when due, and that the said Trustees have the right to cancel this covenant by the payment of One Thousand Dollars.

This Certificate is transferable only on the books of the Seminary.

Oxford, Ohio, September 27th 1865.

COUNTERSIGNED BY

John H. Shuey Treasurer

E. P. Pratt President.

Secretary.

PERMANENT SCHOLARSHIP CERTIFICATE. Hoping to raise money for the seminary, the board of trustees authorized permanent scholarship certificates of $1,000. This certificate from 1856 details its stipulations. It was designed to educate heirs of the holders in perpetuity, one student at a time. Recipients received free board and tuition but agreed to pay for music classes and "warming and lighting of the building."

COLLEGE SEAL. The official seal underwent numerous transformations; however, the Latin phrase *Sigillum Collegii Westernensis* was always inscribed around the outer edge of the circle. Some versions of the seal used the date 1855, when the seminary opened, and others, such as this one, referred to the date of the charter, 1853.

BILLY THE ARK. This affectionate nickname was given to generations of carriages used for transportation by seminary residents. Over the years, each newer version became less "arkish," but the traditional name stuck. The original ark had leather curtains to ensure the privacy of seminary teachers and was a familiar sight on the streets of Oxford.

Two

TIME FOR TRANSITION

EVOLVING FROM SEMINARY TO COLLEGE (1888–1904)

LEILA S. MCKEE. This visionary seminary alumna became its second principal in 1888. With degrees from Wellesley College and Centre College, she modernized the curriculum, increased faculty salaries, expanded the campus, and promoted extracurricular activities, including the introduction of Tree Day and many more of Western's best-loved traditions. In 1894, the trustees renamed the institution The Western: A College and Seminary for Women. Leila McKee was the first person to hold the title of president at Western. She held that position for 10 years, resigning in 1904 to marry James B. Welsh. They moved to Kansas City, Kansas, where she died in 1938. (Photograph by W.N. Breener.)

New Elocution Movement. These students, dressed in gym suits, are training for the exertion of public speaking by engaging in rigorous activities as part of the Delsarte System of Oratory, also called the "New Elocution." Miss McKee fostered this movement at Western and, at a national conference in Cincinnati, Ohio, spoke about the importance of women expressing themselves articulately and persuasively in the public realm.

Class of 1895. The transition to college status brought great expectations for students. New faculty members were added, admission and graduation requirements strengthened, and the curriculum expanded. A college preparatory course, along with classical and literary courses, was added in 1894. Students completing the literary course received diplomas; classical course graduates earned bachelor of arts degrees. (Photograph by Chas. E. Doty.)

Beta Rose. Students and faculty gather on the porch of Peabody Hall, near the rosebush known as the "Beta Rose," in 1896. Leila McKee helped select the rose as the national symbol for Miami's chapter of the Beta Theta Pi social fraternity, founded at Miami University in 1839. Three blooms from this bush were presented at the formal announcement in 1889. This is just one example of Miss McKee's many efforts to maintain a friendly, collegial relationship with students and administrators at neighboring Miami.

Western-Miami Connections. In this 1889 photograph, E.D. Warfield (right), president of Miami University from 1888 to 1891, is seated next to Nellie Tilton, a Western faculty member from 1888 to 1890. She became Mrs. Warfield. The other couple pictured here also married: Walter L. Bridgman, a Miami professor, and Lesline Waterman, of the Western faculty. Socializing between Warfield's all-male "dude faculty" at Miami and Western's all-female faculty was heartily encouraged by Principal McKee. (Photograph by Sargent, Hamilton, Ohio.)

Olivia Brice and Alumnae Hall. An 1866 graduate, Olivia Meily Brice was the first alumna elected to the Western board of trustees. Married to US senator Calvin Brice, she was president of the alumnae association and donated $5,000 for construction of Western's second building. She insisted that it be called Alumnae Hall to recognize all alumnae donors. Dedicated in 1892, the building was designed by Joseph W. Yost and housed a library, laboratory, classrooms, and art studio. Olivia also commissioned a stained-glass window as a memorial to her class. It was designed by Mary Elizabeth Tillinghast and placed in the library. In 1893, the window was exhibited at the World's Fair in Chicago, where it received awards for both design and theme. Alumnae Hall stood until 1977. (Bottom photograph by Frank R. Snyder.)

Art Class. An art class in session shortly after the 1892 dedication of Alumnae Hall uses a male subject for a lesson in portraiture. The instructor (seated to his left), wearing a hat in the fashion of the day, keeps a watchful eye as students sketch on their canvases. The skull on the table in the foreground was used to study the shape of the head and lines of the face.

Calisthenics Class. From the earliest seminary days, the idea of "a sound mind in a sound body" was encouraged, which led to the development of a physical training department. Here, students are shown participating in a calisthenics class in 1891, in which they are completing a dumbbell exercise.

Tennis. By 1890, tennis was extremely popular. Tennis gowns were the new spring fashion, and "love games" and "serves" were common topics of conversation. Courts such as this one near Alumnae Hall were built until 1939, when new clay composition tennis courts were planned on the ground adjoining the hockey field. The first intercollegiate game occurred in 1912, when Hazel Howe (Western) defeated Mary Hayford Morril (Miami) on Miami's court. (Photograph by Frank R. Snyder.)

Department of Physical Training. Initiated in 1894, this department offered academic credit for four years of physical training, as required by Western's curriculum. Students participated in various activities, including tennis, golf, basketball, gymnastics, cycling, weight lifting, and fencing. Faculty members later organized an athletic association to support and oversee students' physical activities.

McKee Hall. The third building constructed on Western's campus, McKee Hall, was completed in 1904. Western's population was growing, and this was the first structure built mainly to house students. President McKee persuaded a neighbor, James R. Patterson, to donate three acres of land for its construction in 1903. Originally called New Hall, it was named for Leila McKee and her father, the Reverend John McKee, a friend and trustee of the college, in 1917.

LAND PURCHASE. In 1904, the trustees acquired a 150-acre tract of land south of Western's campus known as the "Fry Farm." At one point, Western owned a total of five farms where crops and livestock were raised to support the needs of students and faculty.

STUDENT VOLUNTEER CONVENTION. The Student Volunteer Movement for Foreign Missions was dedicated to enlisting Christian college students. Leila McKee (seated center) is shown here with faculty member Anna Miller and students Anne Pearl Beaver and Alice May Sexton, attending the 1892 Student Volunteer Convention in Springfield, Ohio. The previous year, the Oxford group attended the first convention in Cleveland. (Photograph by Millard, Detroit, Michigan.)

Staging the Russian Coronation. Like many Americans, Western faculty, students, and staff were fascinated by the rituals of European royalty. In response to the 1896 coronation of Nicholas II of Russia, the Western community staged a pageant, the "Coronation of Czarina Alexandra." Seen here are Leila McKee depicted as Czarina Alexandra and Miss Lucy Bushnell as her ill-fated husband, Czar Nicholas. (Photograph by Frank R. Snyder, Oxford.)

Clubs and Societies. Though there were no Greek-letter sororities, clubs and societies were very important at Western. Students participated in a number of academic and social organizations, such as the Agora Society, Round Table, Classical Cub, XYZ Club, Mask and Mantle Drama Club, Bread Circle, Dolphin Club, Polliwog Swimming Club, Science Colloquium, and International Relations Club. This photograph shows the 1904 Agora Society, a nationally registered women's club initiated at Western.

Volunteer Band. Begun at Mount Holyoke, the Volunteer Band was part of the International Movement for Foreign Missionaries. In this 1891 photograph, faculty members Elizabeth Crowther and Leila McKee, along with Volunteer Band students, gather at the Spring House. Lucy Dunlap from Thailand (second from right) later found Satriwithaya School in Bangkok. Other religious organizations included the Anywhere Band, Missionary Society, and Christian Endeavor, which organized devotionals, Bible studies, and missionary works. (Photograph by Chas. E. Doty.)

Tree Day Celebration. Transplanted from Wellesley by President McKee, Western's first Tree Day celebration was held in 1890, when this picture was taken. Events included the presentation of spades by the sophomore class to the freshman class, followed by freshmen planting a tree using spades decorated with class colors. Festivities concluded with the raising of class flags, singing class songs, a senior class farewell to its class tree, and most often, a play. Traditionally held in the spring, Tree Day merged with College Day, held in the fall, a more suitable time for planting, in 1956. The flag raising continued to occur in May. (Photograph by Chas. E. Doty.)

The Beechwoods. Rustic and secluded, this was a favorite spot for walks, picnics, and student entertainments. Both students and faculty would go there to socialize and to meditate. Here, the traditional bonfire was lit for Powwow, and many a college song reverberated through the beech trees. The Beechwoods would later be used as a bridle path.

Langstroth Cottage. In 1856, the Reverend Edward Root, minister of Oxford's Second Presbyterian Church and of the seminary, built this house adjacent to the Western campus. In 1859, it became the home of the Reverend Lorenzo Langstroth, inventor of America's first movable-frame beehive. Later, it was owned by Susan Wade Peabody, Helen Peabody's niece, and ultimately by Western College. It then served as a faculty residence and, after 1966, home of the dean of students. In 1976, it was listed in the National Register of Historic Places and, in 1982, designated a National Historic Landmark.

LORENZO LORRAINE LANGSTROTH. Because of his revolutionary invention of the movable-frame beehive, Langstroth was known as the "Father of American Beekeeping." Born in Philadelphia, this apiarist, minister, and teacher moved in 1858 to Oxford, where he devoted his time to beekeeping and experimenting with hives at his home near the Western campus.

***WESTERN-OXFORD* BOARD.** Begun in 1893, the *Western-Oxford* quarterly came to occupy a central place in college life. A joint project of the seminary and its alumnae, it was originally intended to keep the alumnae informed and to make the institution better known. It published important speeches, gave accounts of commencements and social events, and reported news of alumnae branches. Seen here are the 1914 board members.

The Western Oxford.

"HEAR YE NOT THE HUM OF MIGHTY WORKINGS."

VOL. I. OXFORD, OHIO, JANUARY, 1893. NO. 1.

EDITOR, ELLEN WRIGHT THOMAS. ASSOCIATE EDITOR, ANNA WOOD FINLEY.

THE WESTERN OXFORD is published in January and May in the interest of the Alumnæ and Students of the Western Female Seminary, Oxford, Ohio.

TERMS—Fifty cents a year, in advance; Twenty-five cents a number.

Address all letters and communications to

THE WESTERN OXFORD, W. F. S., OXFORD, OHIO.

EDITORIAL.

BEFORE presenting this modest sheet to Seminary friends and Alumnæ, the Editors beg leave to preface a few remarks to indicate the origin, scope and purpose of the Western Oxford.

When the Alumnæ came, last June, from all parts of the world to unite in the dedication of Alumnæ Hall, the complaint arose that the Seminary, as it is today, is not truly known by her students of other days. They know that changes have been made, but what those changes are and what the spirit is that animated them, the Alumnæ feel themselves wholly ignorant of. This little murmur of discontent, the various inquiries implied rather than frankly spoken, and the troubled faces of the

WESTERN-OXFORD QUARTERLY. The first issue appeared in January 1893, using the inspiring slogan, "Hear ye not the hum of mighty workings?" Gradually, the quarterly became an entirely student publication, offering opportunities to publish fiction, essays, or poetry. In 1941, *SCOPE* succeeded the old *Western-Oxford* and featured short stories, poetry, editorials, and artwork.

Dormitory Life. This student room, with its double bed and "Peabody," the sturdy walnut dresser to the left, had a curtained window that admitted light to the closet, also used as a dressing room. These features were typical of student dormitory rooms during Western's early years.

Western College Quartette. Singing was always an important part of life at Western. Seen entertaining on Commencement Day 1897, the Western College Quartette included, from left to right, Mary Moorehead, of Xenia, Ohio; Hattie Wishard, of Ogden, Utah; Jennie McElroy, of Liberty, Indiana; and Annie Packard, of Decatur, Illinois. Their chant was, "Who, who, who are we? We are the jolly AKE!"

Three

Golden Jubilee
Prospering and Growing (1904–1914)

Lilian Wyckoff Johnson. The first woman to receive a doctoral degree at Cornell University (in 1902), Lilian Wyckoff Johnson served as Western's president from 1904 to 1906. Despite her short tenure, Dr. Johnson is credited with organizing Western's 1905 Golden Jubilee celebration. Illness forced her to resign in 1906.

Senior Day. On February 2, 1905, Western observed its first official Senior Day as these seniors attended classes in their caps and gowns. Tradition and continuity were important at Western, and freshmen also had their own special day of recognition. It had become common for them to display their chosen class colors in the fall. President Johnson designated this day as "College Day," held on president emeritus Leila McKee's birthday, October 9.

Clara Pierce and Domestic Science. Clara Pierce served as the first head of the department of domestic Science, which began in 1903 and offered classes on such subjects as dietetics and cooking. Western was one of the first American colleges to offer academic credit for domestic science. The program later became the department of home economics.

East Cottage. Built in 1859 as the seminary steward's home, this house was renamed East Cottage in 1906 and used as a model home for domestic science and, later, home economics students. For many years, it also housed the infirmary, which replaced the variously located sick rooms of earlier days. In 1929–1930, the college physician lectured freshmen on personal hygiene and seniors on parenthood. (Photograph by George R. Hoxie.)

The Golden Jubilee

and

The Fiftieth

Annual Commencement

of

The Western College for Women

Oxford, Ohio

Golden Jubilee Celebration

June Sixth, 1905

2:00 P. M.

College Campus

Golden Jubilee, 1905. In 1904, anticipating the Golden Jubilee 50th anniversary, alumnae and trustees created a $50,000 Helen Peabody Endowment Fund, which included support for a new gymnasium and a Helen Peabody Chair of Biblical History and Literature. Activities during the yearlong celebration also included academic programs, talks by prominent visiting scholars, events for students and alumnae, and publication of a book of alumnae recollections.

... Constitution ...

—of—

The Student Government League

—of—

The Western College

Oxford, Ohio

1907

STUDENT GOVERNMENT LEAGUE. Organized in 1907, the student government league allowed students, with faculty support, to experience self-government. It helped draft a student constitution, choose a student governing board, and select the first student body president. Here were sown the seeds of Western's honor system, with its inherent ideals of individual honor and responsibility. Dean Alma Sawyer, as acting president, rendered a grant of powers for students to govern themselves, and the league joined the National Organization of Student Governments.

LEAGUE ACTIVITIES. League activities included managing the student kitchen in Peabody Hall and maintaining quiet during study hours. In 1914, the league officers shown here sponsored teas during exam week. Lucy Kent, voice instructor, sang in the Agora room, which was decorated with the Western flag, candles, and daffodils to create a restful setting meant to soothe fatigue.

John Grant Newman. In 1908, John Grant Newman became the first male president of Western. President Newman was known for his success in securing donations for the college's Living Endowment Fund. He also worked to raise academic standards, reorganize the faculty, and establish a faculty promotion system. President Newman resigned in 1912 to become pastor of Chambers Wylie Presbyterian Church in Philadelphia, Pennsylvania.

The Western *Multifaria*. First published by the seniors, this yearbook appeared in 1910. Its initial volume was dedicated to President Newman. In subsequent years, the junior class produced the yearbook. The *Multifaria* (meaning "telling of many things") chronicled the year's activities with photographs of organizations, extracurricular activities, academic classes, faculty, staff, and students.

EDGAR AND JESSIE STILLMAN KELLEY. In 1910, leading American composer Dr. Edgar Stillman Kelley and his wife, accomplished singer and pianist Jessie Gregg Kelley, came to Western. Jessie became director of piano music, and Edgar received the nation's first resident fellowship for creative work. While at Western, he enjoyed his most prolific period, producing his most famous work. From 1923 to 1934, Jessie directed Western's music program and served as president of the Ohio Federation of Music Clubs, National Federation of Music Clubs, and Ohio Music Teachers' Association. The Kelleys retired in 1934 but continued to reside in Oxford when not traveling. Edgar died in 1944 and Jessie in 1949. (Photographs by Jacobi Studio, Hamilton, Ohio.)

STILLMAN KELLEY STUDIO. This cozy studio home was designed for Dr. Edgar and Jessie Stillman Kelley and completed in 1916. The class of 1916, for whom Edgar was the faculty sponsor, donated and raised funds for the one-and-a-half-story bungalow, located on the west side of campus.

Part One

THE

Pilgrim's Progress

A Musical Miracle Play

Music by

Edgar Stillman Kelley

Op. 37

KELLEY'S WORKS. Dr. Edgar Kelley's first composition in the new studio was *Pilgrim's Progress*, an oratorio performed in 1918 that is considered his greatest work. While in Oxford, he also composed his second symphony, the *New England Symphony*, first performed in 1913, and wrote the *Alice in Wonderland* suite, which was performed in 1919. A tone poem, "The Pit and the Pendulum," premiered at the May Festival in Cincinnati on May 9, 1925, when it was awarded "Best New American Work for Orchestra" by the National Federation of Music Clubs.

MARY ALMA SAWYER. Helen Peabody hired Mary Alma Sawyer in 1887 as an instructor in chemistry and physics. In 1895, Western trustees approved Sawyer's promotion to the newly created position of dean, which she held until retiring in 1920. She served as acting president from 1906 to 1908 and from 1912 to 1914. During her presidencies, the student government league was formed, the faculty adopted a new grading system, and the East Cottage model home opened. (Photograph by W.N. Breener.)

SAWYER GYMNASIUM. Named for Dean Mary Alma Sawyer to recognize her efforts in securing its construction in 1914, this state-of-the-art gymnasium featured a variety of fitness apparatus, including horizontal ladders, stall bars, climbing ropes, flying and traveling rings, chest weights and expanders, and rowing machines. It was also equipped to support gymnastic exercises, basketball, volleyball, and other indoor games. (Photograph by James N. Keen.)

SAWYER POOL. Dean Sawyer allegedly encouraged students to swim in the Tallawanda Creek as a strategy to persuade Western trustees to include a pool during construction of the gymnasium. Shown here in 1917, the pool was available for recreational use and also served student clubs, such as the synchronized swimming team and the Dolphins. (Photograph by F.H. Haskett.)

ROUND TABLE. Organized in February 1903, this club became a member of the Ohio Federation of Clubs. The aims of Round Table were to study current affairs and the latest movements in modern art, as well as read modern literature. In 1910, Round Table students held a debate on the controversial topic "Immigration to the United States."

Summer House. Built by 1860, the Summer House was located on the path from Peabody Green to the pond. The small shelter is depicted on the original grounds plan in the 1856 catalog. This photograph shows students and faculty using it as a place for relaxation and fellowship. The corner posts, fashioned from tree branches, were replaced with stone in the mid-1930s.

Student Dining. For students and faculty dining in the basement of Peabody Hall in February 1909, dinner was an elegant event. They were seated at tables formally adorned with linen cloths and place settings and politely waited to be served. This practice lasted until family-style, and finally, cafeteria-style dining became the custom.

Four

The Great War vs. Roaring Twenties

Building Bridges (1914–1931)

William Waddell Boyd. As president from 1914 to 1931, William Waddell Boyd oversaw a period of steady growth. The domestic work system was dropped, assets grew, a faculty pension plan was introduced, and the number of faculty and students increased. During his presidency, Ernst Nature Theatre, Kumler Memorial Chapel, Presser Hall, Sawyer Gymnasium, Western Lodge, and Western's 10 signature stone bridges were built.

PATTERSON PLACE. In 1898, James Patterson built this summer home known as Glenwilde on 70 acres just south of Western Drive. After his death, Patterson's sisters donated the home to Western, at which point it was modernized and became the year-round residence of the college's presidents from 1914 to 1974. President Boyd and his family were the first to occupy it. Today, Patterson Place Museum houses the Western College Alumnae Association offices, Narka Nelson Archives, and artifacts and memorabilia of Western College.

19 MULTI FARIA 16

The Sixtieth Commencement of the Western College for Women

HOW can an epochal celebration be caught into speech and preserved for the remembrance of this generation? The Sixtieth Commencement of The Western College for Women was epochal. Preparations for the celebration had begun early; the enthusiasm was contagious; great anticipation made the thrills of that week like no other since The Western began. Old girls' "hearts that beat like sixty" planned to flock home to the college for The Glorious Sixtieth. Dreams long cherished were realized in that memorable home-coming. Three members of the fiftieth reunion class were present; one of the fifty-fifth.

The events of the Week? I assure you, just being here and seeing folks was an event. Always Commencement is this way, but the Sixtieth was sixty times more so. "Why, there's 'Pa' Wade!" "Well, Candace, I didn't know *you* were coming!" "Oh, Mary, you dear girl!" They forgot that they were mothers of large families and belonged to a thirtieth or fortieth reunion class. They were simply Western girls again. This at first made some of the undergraduates feel like the freshmen, who come in September and hear the shrieks of joy that accompany ecstatic conjunctions of old girls. But soon new acquaintances were made with these other Western girls, unknown before.

For the entertainment of the Western "homeseekers," Petruchio and Kate acted their shrewish and delightful parts under the maples and The House of Rimmon met its dire fate on the same enchanted spot. To greet the first guests, a French comedy was given, needing no translation save the clever acting. On Baccalaureate Sabbath, there were the joys of quiet strolls with old friends, the beautiful morning service, full of the dignity of the Western manner of worship, the class prayer-meetings in unusual spots in the sunset glow, and the interesting vespers. The Commencement concert, the president's reception at Patterson Place, the 1915 Step Exercises — all these were occasions to promote that fine fellowship which characterized the Sixtieth. Never before was there such an alumnae banquet — a banquet held in the gymnasium, where daisies from the Daisy Field twined the ropes and where songs

SIXTIETH COMMENCEMENT. In 1916, Western celebrated 60 years of educating young women with a reunion of Western classes. The celebration included the performance of a French comedy, worship services, a commencement concert, and president's reception. It culminated with an alumnae banquet in Sawyer Hall, where the songs and cheers of trustees and students reportedly resounded from the rafters.

WAR PROGRAM. In 1915, students in middy blouses sit in the Peabody senior parlor, knitting in preparation for possible American involvement in the European war. Western administrators, faculty, staff, and students showed their growing concern with such efforts, and classes were offered on first aid, engine repair, stenography, typewriting, French, gardening, and sewing.

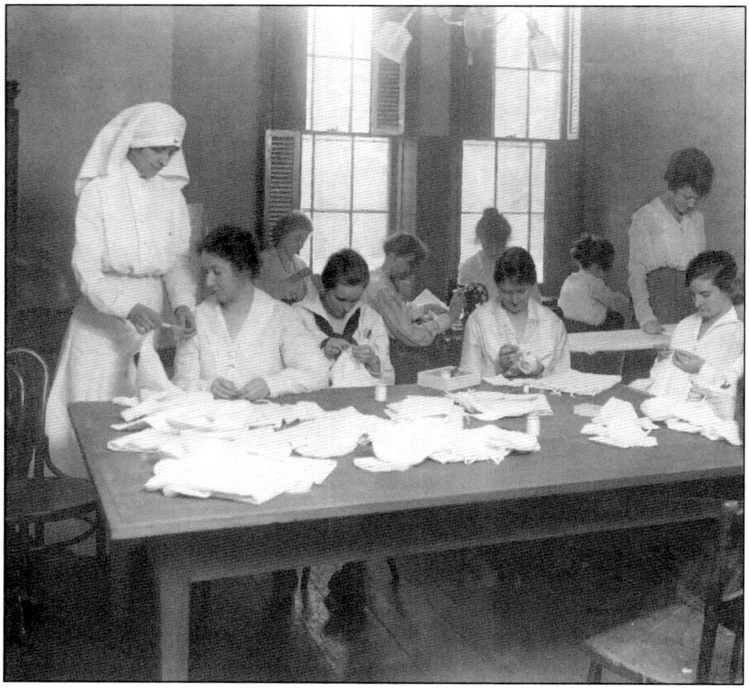

War Efforts. Shown here in 1917 shortly after the United States entered World War I, Western students joined a newly organized Red Cross unit. Students met weekly to prepare surgical dressings, pads, and compresses and to attend lectures on first aid by resident physician Dr. Mary Denton. Along with other colleges, Western did its part to support the troops.

Influenza Outbreak. In fall 1918, visitors were not admitted to Western grounds because of the Spanish flu outbreak, a pandemic ultimately responsible for more deaths worldwide than the Great War. The quarantine lasted five weeks, the number of flu cases was limited to two students, and no one died.

INFLUENZA RECOVERY. Western was spared the worst of the pandemic that swept across the United States and beyond. Students pictured here are celebrating Western's good fortune, dressed as a bottle of mouthwash and pill bottles! One student is holding a "doctor's bag" to encourage good hygiene in order to avoid spreading the dreaded flu.

BARRACKS. In 1919, the Barracks, an *L*-shaped wing attached to the south side of Sawyer Gymnasium, was constructed to alleviate a student housing shortage. In 1934, the structure was renovated and renamed the Cottage. In 1943, the infirmary was moved here from East Cottage, and still later, it became Hillside. Over the years, this building was truly multipurpose: infirmary, dormitory, student union, faculty apartments, and guesthouse. Although Sawyer Gymnasium was spared, the annex was razed in 1974.

Organized labor favors building of municipal light plant

THE LOWEST PRICE

LET US SHOW THEM TO YOU

HAMILTON EVENING JOURNAL

Largest Circulation Guaranteed

36,000

12 PAGES

WEATHER

FAIR TONIGHT AND THURSDAY; TEMPERATURE UNCHANGED.

WEDNESDAY, AUGUST 18, 1920

24,000,000 WOMEN GIVEN SUFFRAGE RIGHT

POLES DRIVE BACK THE RUSSIAN HORDES

INSURRECTION PLANNED

In Korea When the Americans Arrive

GARD IN PARTY

Of Congressmen Now In the Orient

PONZI ON HIS WAY TO JAIL

Counter-Offensive Clears Danzig Corridor of Soviet Troops.

Peace Delegates Hold Their First Meeting—National Existence of Poland Recognized.

DIRECTS BUREAU IN LABOR DEPARTMENT

Miss Mary Anderson.

TENNESSEE LEGISLATURE PASSED FEDERAL AMENDMENT TODAY

Final Vote In Titanic Struggle Was 49 to 47—Effort To Table Indorsement Resolution Failed

Epitome of Women's Battle for Suffrage.

Women's Suffrage Movement. This headline from the August 16, 1920, issue of the *Hamilton Evening Journal* celebrates the right to vote. Women's suffrage in the United States was achieved in 1920 with the passage of the 19th Amendment to the US Constitution. In 1911 and 1912, the Western Suffragette Society and Western College Equal Suffrage worked for the cause. (Courtesy of Smith Library of Regional History.)

Two Deans. Two strong and legendary women shared the office of dean through the 1920s and 1930s. Alice Hill Byrne (right), a Wellesley graduate and associate professor of Latin and Greek, served as academic dean. Anna Helen Tappan, a 1909 Western graduate and professor of mathematics, served first as dean of women, then succeeded Dean Byrne in 1941.

Western Farms. The college owned five farms of various sizes over the course of its history. Four in Oxford raised corn, wheat, pork, and dairy cows; one in Georgetown, Ohio, raised tobacco. In 1915, Pres. William Boyd invited the Farmers' Protection Association to the college to offer suggestions on how to make the farms profitable; however, they eventually became a financial liability and were sold.

Farmerettes. Seen here in 1918, Farmerettes and Western's farmer are hard at work. By this time, the Western College Farm Service unit had begun, permitting student members to substitute farm work for gymnasium classes. They planted and harvested crops, canned food, and cared for campus grounds.

Chapel Services. Beginning in 1871 and until the construction of Kumler Memorial Chapel in 1918, daily chapel was held in the south wing of Seminary (later, Peabody) Hall, the space today occupied by Leonard Theatre. Church services and other special programs were also held there. This photograph shows faculty seated on the platform, near the students. The organ pipes can be seen in the middle of the picture.

Kumler Memorial Chapel. Dedicated in 1918, Kumler Chapel was a gift of 1879 alumna Anna Kumler Wight and her sister, Ella Kumler McKelvy, to honor their parents and paternal grandfather. This interior photograph shows the chancel and pulpit during a service. With the exception of annual alumnae weekend reunions, no regular chapel or church services have been held here since 1974. It remains a popular venue for special events, such as concerts, lectures, graduations, and weddings.

The Reverend Jeremiah Prophet Elias Kumler. The Reverend Jeremiah Kumler, later a member and president of the Western board of trustees, married Abbie Goulding, a member of Western's original faculty. They were considered loving friends of the college. The 1917 *Multifaria* was dedicated to Western's "first couple."

Tillinghast Window. The class of 1866 presented this stained-glass window as part of the dedication of the beautiful new Alumnae Hall at commencement in June 1892. Created by prominent New York artist Mary Tillinghast and titled *The Sweet Graduate*, it symbolizes the new image of strong, independent women emerging in the 1890s. First installed in the Alumnae Hall library, it was exhibited at the 1893 Chicago World's Fair, damaged after a second exhibition at the 1933 World's Fair, and not reinstalled until 1981, when it was restored and placed in Kumler Chapel.

Choir and Glee Club. In this 1899 photograph, members of the glee club pose in the student parlor. Music was always part of Western tradition, and choir and glee club membership was open to qualified students from all classes. Choir performed regularly at chapel and church services and, as did various other musical groups, at college events. Students enjoyed occasional exchange concerts when the Western Choir joined with choirs from other colleges, especially all-male Wabash and Kenyon. Special performances in later years included appearing with the Cincinnati Symphony Orchestra and singing on Cincinnati's WLW radio.

Western Pond and Ice House. Students in 1900 take a leisurely walk "on the avenue" past the Ice House. Built around 1859 next to this natural pond, it was located along the original carriage road that ended in front of Peabody Hall and was used to store ice for the kitchen. A boathouse later replaced it. During cold winters, skaters enjoyed the frozen surface.

Original Bridges. Though these students seem to be enjoying the wooden bridges of early days, President Boyd and the trustees sought to improve the Western campus. In search of beauty and functionality, they turned to Cephas Burns, a local stonemason.

Stone Bridges and Lampposts. Cephas Burns worked at Western College from 1914 to 1931. With his team of workers, Burns replaced the wood bridges with distinctive stone bridges, utilizing cannonball stones from Tallawanda Creek, Collins Run, and Harker's Run. The Burns team was also responsible for stone lampposts, stonework on the Summer House, the Lookout on the pond, stonework of Kumler Chapel and Stillman Kelley Studio, the stone foundation and fireplace of Western Lodge, the original Ernst Nature Theatre, Corson House, Stancote House, and Grey Gables.

Cephas A. Burns. Born the grandson of freed slaves, Cephas Burns lived from 1871 to 1935. He learned masonry from his father, and one of his commissions came from President Boyd, who directed him to replace Western's wooden footbridges with those made of stone. He was the master builder of stonework that graces not only the Western campus but other structures in Oxford as well. Burns was a prominent Oxford resident and a member of Bethel AME Church. (Courtesy of Smith Library of Regional History.)

ERNST NATURE THEATRE. A US senator from Kentucky and Western trustee, Richard P. Ernst donated funds for this outdoor amphitheater. It was designed by landscape architects Olmsted Brothers of Brookline, Massachusetts, and built in 1921 by local workers under the careful supervision of President Boyd and theater professor Gertrude Leonard. Placed on two facing natural slopes, it was planned with no buildings, posts, or statues. It was dedicated on Tree Day, May 23, 1922, and opened with the play *Prunella*, directed by Professor Leonard, who had led the appeal for funds. Ernst Nature Theatre was used for college ceremonies, concerts, festivals, and every kind of play, from Greek tragedy to Shakespeare to modern drama. A bird sanctuary, developed nearby as a special project of Leonard, attracted more than 100 varieties of birds over the years.

SEN. RICHARD P. ERNST. A US senator from Kentucky (1921–1927), Richard P. Ernst served on the Western board of trustees from 1890 to 1933. Born in Covington, Kentucky, he graduated from Centre College in 1878, received his law degree from the Cincinnati Law School in 1880, and practiced law in Cincinnati. An early advocate of women's rights, he was made an honorary member of the class of 1923 because of his deep interest in the welfare and activities of the college.

CORSON HOUSE. Built in 1923 by Dr. Oscar T. and Ella Corson, this was the first of three houses built with the understanding that they would eventually become Western property. Used by Western as a residence for retired faculty, Corson House was located south of Western Drive, near the Clark Memorial Gateway. It was converted into faculty apartments in 1955 and razed in 1977.

Mary Lyon Hall. Completed in June 1925, this dormitory was named in honor of Mary Lyon in 1934 to acknowledge Western's relationship with Mount Holyoke and its founder. The building is located west of McKee Hall on ground donated by the Patterson estate and is one of Western's five dormitories, all of which are still used as residence halls by Miami University.

Mary Lyon. Mary Lyon was a pioneer in women's education. She established the Wheaton Female Seminary in Norton, Massachusetts, and in 1837, Mount Holyoke Female Seminary in South Hadley, Massachusetts, where she served as the first principal. Her influential vision fused intellectual challenge, moral purpose, and practical affordability, helping shape 19th-century women's education. Lyon, an instructor and mentor of Helen Peabody at Mount Holyoke, was also a friend of Western's founders, Daniel and Mary Tenney. (Photograph courtesy of Mount Holyoke College Archive Special Collections.)

Heath Chime. Given in 1925 by Elizabeth McCullough Heath, an 1884 graduate, the set of 11 bells was placed in the tower of Alumnae Hall. Following the building's demolition, the chime was restored and hung in the Molyneaux-Western Tower erected to house it. The bells have a musical range of one note over an octave and are engraved with excerpts of poetry by Alfred, Lord Tennyson.

Dr. John Molyneaux. Distinguished Oxford citizen, Western College trustee from 1914 until his death in 1953, and acting president in the spring and summer of 1941, John Molyneaux and his family were among the college's oldest and most loyal friends. A grant from the Molyneaux Foundation was responsible for the restoration of the Heath Chime and construction of the bell tower.

Western Lodge. The lodge was a gift from Col. A.E. Humphreys, a friend of Elizabeth McCullough Heath and her husband, Fletcher Heath. In 1925, Humphreys sent logs from Colorado for the building, which was modeled after his hunting lodge in the Rocky Mountains. Stonemason Cephas Burns laid the foundation and constructed the large fireplace and chimney. The lodge served as headquarters of the YWCA and, later, as a student recreation center. (Photograph by Robert C. Crow.)

Grey Gables. In 1930, President Boyd built Grey Gables as a post-presidency residence. He departed Oxford shortly thereafter, and the home became, first, a guest house and, later, a restaurant. Miami University purchased it in 1958, using it for temporary housing, then for offices. In 1967, it was moved 45 feet south to the northwest corner of Chestnut Street and Patterson Avenue.

PRESSER HALL. Built in 1931 for the music department, this stately graystone building had offices, practice rooms, and studios for both music and art departments. Its spacious Edgar and Jessie Stillman Kelley Auditorium was used for important events, such as presidential inaugurations, concerts, commencements, and other noteworthy occasions. The Theodore Presser Foundation contributed half the construction cost. This was Western's only academic building facing Patterson Avenue.

Lincoln Memorial Essay Contest. Dr. Oscar Corson, who owned a large Abraham Lincoln library, established the Lincoln Memorial Essay Contest. He offered a $50 prize every presidential election year to the Western student who wrote the best essay on Lincoln. In February 1929, following the 1928 election of Pres. Herbert Hoover, Eva Schwidetsky, a German student, was awarded the prize for her essay, "Lincoln and His Cabinet."

Peabody Cup. Western celebrated its 75th anniversary in June 1930. Records show that 7,010 students had attended since the seminary opened in 1855. The class of 1880, celebrating its 50th reunion with 12 of 19 class members present, received the Susan W. Peabody Cup, a silver trophy awarded to the class with the largest percentage of surviving members in attendance.

Needham Prizes. These happy winners of Needham Prizes benefited from a gift of $2,000 from Charles Needham of Louisville, Kentucky, emphasizing Western's principle of "sound mind in sound body." At the beginning of each year, $25 was awarded to the five freshmen judged to be in the best physical condition ("perfect babies") and, at the end of the year, another five who had improved the most ("better babies"). The three Needham Prize winners with the best scholastic record during their sophomore year received an additional award.

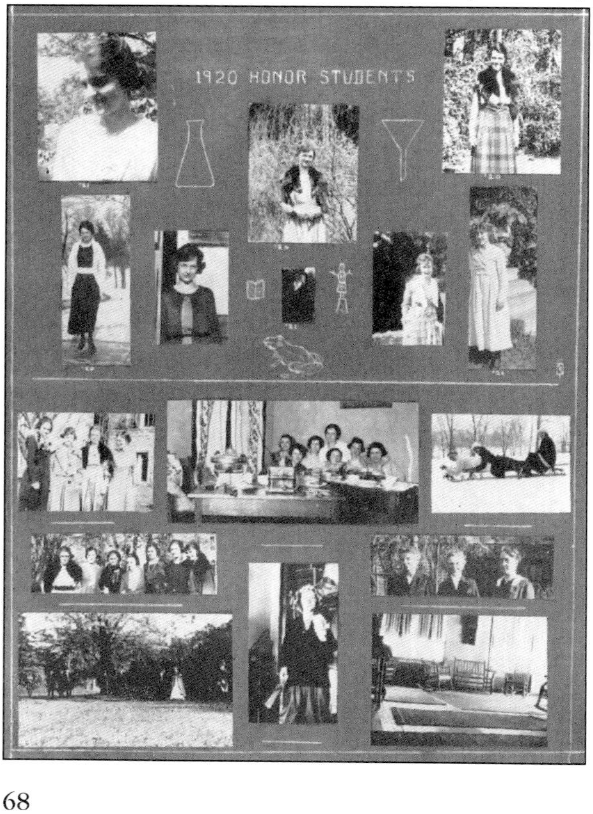

Honor Society. Founded in 1914 in accordance with the standards of the national Phi Beta Kappa society, the honor society recognized excellence in scholarship and service to the college community. It represented the highest academic honor the college could bestow. Membership included the president, dean, faculty who were members of Phi Beta Kappa or Sigma Psi, and Western College graduates after 1908 who had received senior honors. Of undergraduates, up to one-fourth of the senior class and three members of the junior class were eligible for election.

Red Cross Lifesaving Corps. Western organized a Red Cross Lifesaving Corps in 1925. Students served as lifeguards, presented water pageants, and taught lifesaving methods in the gymnasium pool. The corps conducted all Red Cross Lifesaving tests and became one of the most active units in the country. President Boyd (right) served as honorary president; Margaret Bogart (left) was the instructor.

International Club. Pictured in 1930, members of the international club included students from Chile, China, India, France, Germany, and Uganda. Members considered themselves daughters of the world and eagerly followed world affairs, adopting the motto, "Nothing which happens in the world is alien to me." The highlight of 1930 was a presentation by League of Nations representative M. Pierre de Lanux, speaking on whether the United States should enter the league.

Art Club. Formed in 1919, the art club encouraged art appreciation among members and students, sponsoring exhibits of works by prominent national artists. Club members traveled to Cincinnati museums and, when permitted, also viewed private collections. In April 1931, an exhibit of Gustave Baumann prints was displayed in the art studio.

Bird Club. In 1934, bird club members place feeders in trees behind Peabody Hall hoping to attract "feathered friends." Organized in 1932, the club recruited students interested in ornithology. Meetings often consisted of walks around campus to watch for rare birds, such as white robins and red-breasted nuthatches. Other activities included decorating trees with suet, cranberries, and raw peanuts.

Bobbed Hair Club. The "bob" haircut became popular among American women in the 1920s and was regarded as a somewhat shocking statement of independence. In 1922, Western women caught the hair craze, and students are seen here showing off their bobs. Across campus, they wanted to be known as *Sorores in Academicae*, or "Sisters of the Academy," and as "Those who have been shorn." Their motto was "Down with Hair Pins!"

Stillman Kelley Music Club. Organized in 1923 by members of the music department, the club's chief object was to promote student interest in good music. Members had the opportunity to enjoy evenings in the Kelleys' home and the privilege of associating with one of America's foremost composers and his wife. Members of the club are seen here in 1925 with Kelley (center front).

Oxford Depot. Although Western expected to have railroad connections before the seminary opened in 1855, the railroad through Oxford was not completed until 1859. Oxford's train station was on the northwest corner of South Elm Street and West Spring Street. It ran from Hamilton to Oxford to Rushville, Indiana, connecting two north-south railroads: the Cincinnati-Hamilton-Dayton Railroad and the Rushville-Indianapolis-Chicago line. Regular passenger service ended in 1950, although "specials" for students continued for several more years.

Five

Financial Challenges
Maintaining Academic Strength (1931–1941)

Ralph Kiddoo Hickok. Former pastor and professor of biblical literature and history at Wells College, Dr. Hickok presided over Western from 1931 to 1941, guiding the college through the Great Depression. He revised the curriculum and initiated three levels of cum laude distinction. Orientation week was added to the calendar, and regulations for smoking, dancing, and chaperoning were relaxed. Sadly, with much still to be accomplished, President Hickok suffered a serious heart attack and was forced to resign. (Photograph by Nickolas Boris.)

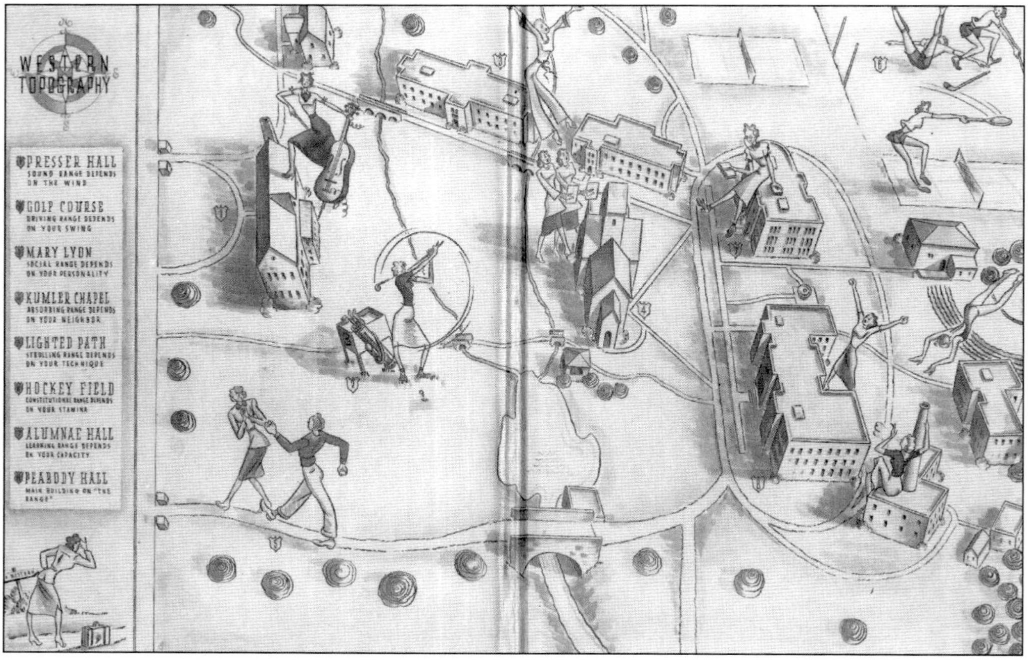

Strategic Cartography. This lighthearted look at Western from 1938 shows both buildings and popular uses of the campus. At lower left, a student enters campus and envisions what she will see during her tour: sports, music, and academic pursuits. Although living through the Great Depression was a difficult experience, Western launched an aggressive marketing campaign that helped fund needed improvements.

The Great Depression. Group photography was associated with 19th- and 20th-century colleges for women in the United States. At Western, this began when Helen Peabody posed with the entire faculty and student body on the steps of Peabody Hall as early as 1858. From September 28, 1932, this photograph shows President Hickok with faculty and students

GERMAN CLUB. The smiling faces of these students in 1933 belie the woeful state of national and international economies. The *Multifaria* noted that the club spent much of its time that year discussing Adolf Hitler's "New Germany."

in front of Kumler Memorial Chapel, during a time when the college was facing financial challenges and a dwindling student body. In 1932, trustees imposed a 10 percent reduction in salaries of Western faculty and staff. Helen Peabody's mantra, "Masters of the situation anywhere," echoed as the college withstood tough times.

THE *QUESTION MARK* AND *ROUND-UP*. Students hard at work on the next issue of *Round-Up* show dedication to their newspapers. The *Question Mark*, produced by the YWCA, published its first issue on October 4, 1930, to represent the student point of view and offer information about social events in Oxford, the United States, and the world. This continued in the *Western Roundup* (later, *Round-Up*), first published in September 1931. The *Western Weekly* replaced *Round-Up* in 1971 and continued until 1974. (Photograph by George R. Hoxie.)

The Question Mark

VOL. I, NO. 2 WESTERN COLLEGE, OXFORD, O. OCTOBER 11, 1930

COLLEGE DAY$

On Tuesday, October 14th we will celebrate the birthday of Leila S. McKee, former president of Western College. It is interesting to look back into the history of College Day and see how it grew from a modest birthday celebration to the elaborate occasion which it has become. Fortunately the old Western Ox fords gave much space to college festivities and we have accounts of Miss McKee's birthday, in almost every autumn number.

In the December 1894 number of Western Oxford we find that October 9 was the occasion for a costume party at tea, representing "All Sorts and Conditions of Men." In 1895 the celebration took the form of "an hour in the woods from 2:30 to 3:30." The girls were photographed against the beautiful autumnal background, says Western Oxford. In 1896 Miss McKee gave an inspiring chapel talk. This talk seems to have become a yearly custom, for mention of it is made every year during Miss McKee's residence at Western. A surprise for Miss McKee was brought about by the students, as they marched out of chapel. They sang an original song to her to the tune of "The Red, White and Blue."

In 1900 a half holiday for celebrating was given the students. The afternoon was spent "walking to Woods Station, taking a hay ride to High Banks, a bicycle trip to College Corner, or a walk down the Reily Road. "The birthday celebration of 1901 was postponed due to rain and was finally held in the Biology Laboratory. There were fortune tellers, marshmallows to toast and dancing. The girls dressed as gypsies and prizes were given for the costumes.

In 1903 a picnic supper in the beech woods was held. This was the beginning of that custom which is still in vogue. The Glee Club sang around a blazing fire and class yells were exchanged.

In 1904 we have the first mention of College Day guests. The Western Oxford describes guests in great numbers arriving by train. This year the beech woods picnic was held at noon as it is today and the first basketball game between the Sophomores and the Freshmen was introduced.

In 1910 the present chapel service was instigated. The Freshmen marched in as they do now, wearing their colors for the first time. The basketball game by this time had become traditional and there was much excitement as to the outcome. There are vague allusions to the dress worn by the players which indicate that it was rather more cumbersome than that of today. Floats were presented by the Sophomores, giving historical sketches of college life before 1910.

Our College Day on Tuesday will be a more elaborate occasion than that of the old times. We no longer have Miss McKee's annual chapel talk which seemed to be so great an inspiration to the students of her administration. Our message this year will come from the Honorable Rennie Smith.

The Freshmen will display their colors and the Perfect Babies will be announced. As usual we will have our luncheon in the beech woods and the basketball game afterward. Monday night, preceding College Day, the Pow-wow will be held, at which the classes will struggle to outdo each other in song and verse. Although none of these activities made up the original College Day, we hope that a few of us will remember Miss McKee for whom the festivities are given. The present Junior and Senior classes had the pleasure of seeing and meeting Miss McKee, now Mrs. Welsh, during the year 1928-1929. A Western Oxford correspondent of 1897 describes her as a Southern lady with unusual executive ability, tall and handsome, with bright dark eyes and a soft voice, "guiltless of the r". Her ancestry goes back to Robert Bruce, the Western Oxford tells us. Miss McKee was our second college president, succeeding Miss Peabody. For her our present "McKee" dormitory is named.

Page 4 THE QUESTION MARK October 4th, 1930

Social and Personal

As the result of injuries received in Hamilton, Alberta McGee, a Freshman, returned to her home at Martin's Ferry, Ohio. She will be back at Western in about ten days. Her friends hope for her quick recovery.

We've heard it rumored that several of the students are chagrined at having received a notice for a Biology fee of five dollars. Inasmuch as the constant use of the microscope strains the eye considerably, thereby necessitating eye-treatment or even glasses, it is expected that many Biol students will ask that they be allowed to contribute the amount for this cause.

On the evening of October the second, President Boyd attended an Alumnae meeting held at the home of Mrs. Ruth Walker, Sycamore, Indiana.

Dot Vehslage and Pat Smith are planning to entertain several of their friends at tea, Sunday, in New Dorm. The guests will include the Misses Ruth Allen, Willie Pister, Helen Basinger, Babs Harrison, Mary Elizabeth Duffield and Mary Beth Forbes.

There has been a great deal of marching in the corridors of P. H. Perhaps, for the good of all concerned, we should suggest that the Gym may be reached by going out any of the back doors and following the road or sidewalk.

You've all heard of the meanest man, the Scotchman, who, with shotgun, went outdoors on Christmas Eve, fired once, and then told his children that he had shot Santa Claus and they could therefore expect no presents. But, compared to two Sophs he was really very kind-hearted. Imagine two Western girls, cruel-hearted enough to ask an unknowing Freshman bell-girl to page two people and giving their own names.

The Misses Betty Ray, Isabelle Jones, Peg Jones and Ginney Chamberlain spent a lovely day in Cincy on Monday. The adjective "lovely" seems vague, but that was all the information we could get.

Living on the fourth floor of Peabody may have its advantages but it is no easier to take a sneak light cut up there than anywhere else. If you don't believe us ask a well-known basketball player who might have sustained serious injuries in her attempt to elude the house-chairman.

The modern spirit invades even the Lit notebooks. An excerpt from one of them, recently handed in to Miss Alkire, in which the author describes the Celtic woman, follows:

"She was wise, industrious and docile and she loved her man."

Isabelle Jones and Ginney Chamberlain were planning to entertain a few friends by having a slumber party Saturday night, but the guest list grew out of all proportion to their room and plans were abandoned. Of course we wouldn't suggest the Agora roof.

Ruth Ward, like a good many of us, was a bit sceptical of perfect bridge hands, until she was dealt one, recently. She held four aces, four kings, four queens and a Jack, but the elation was short-lived. No sooner had she played the hand than she discovered that the cards had been stacked. It's not often they are stacked in such a manner.

Last Monday Miss Howe, in company with Lillian Olivella, Maria Morales, Flora Davila and Alice Baudaut, motored to Cincinnati to shop. They lunched at the Hotel Gibson and it is said that the table conversation was carried on in Spanish.

Fall Elections

There have been several new officers elected since school opened this Fall, as well as some office refilled due to the absence of students who were elected last year.

Parliament has a good-sized list of new officials for this year. The Senior representatives are Rosemary Ferguson and Helen Banister. The various floor chairmen of the different halls are also Parliament members. Those of Peabody Hall are Wilma Hartley, Catherine Ratcliffe, and Helen Johansen; of McKee, Helen Clarke; of Barracks, Mary Agnes Travis; and of New Dormitory, Helen McGregor. The Junior Class has as its representatives Leslie Van Cleve, Mary Louise Ellerbusch, Mary Rude Stevenson, and Mary Delp, who is Secretary of Parliament. From the Sophomore Class, Parliament has taken Elizabeth Ward, Josephine Van Ness, Lou Leonard, and Pat Ryan.

The returns from other elections on the campus are as follows: Susan Baker is president of the Sophomore Class, taking Eleanor Slingluff's place; Mary Mason has been chosen to lead the school in song this year. Marian White is the new captain of the Life Saving Corps and Roberta Treneer is the secretary of the Athletic Association. In Y. W., Abby Bryant has been appointed as Social Service Chairman.

CURRICULUM REVISION. By 1933, students at Western were required to maintain a "C" average. A committee undertook intensive study and revision of the curriculum that led to decreasing requirements and greater elective freedom. Dean Alice Byrne announced a list of new courses: experimental, social, and abnormal psychology; scientific German; criminology and penology; money and banking; poverty dependency; genetics; and population and race problems.

REQUIREMENTS FOR THE DEGREE OF BACHELOR OF ARTS

Candidates for the degree of Bachelor of Arts must complete at least 124 semester hours of work, with a C average on all work credited. One semester hour is equivalent to one academic appointment a week for one semester. Four credit points an hour are assigned to a grade of A, three to a grade of B, two to a grade of C and one to a grade of D. To obtain the C average a student must have twice as many credit points as she has semester hours. The requirement of 124 semester hours includes 4 semester hours of work in Physical Education. An additional requirement for graduation is the passing of the test in swimming described on page 82. Exemption may be secured only through the college physician. Students who are excused from swimming will be expected to continue work in the department of Physical Education until they have completed the four semester hours required.

The curriculum is designed to insure each student a well-rounded, general education. To guard against too early and too narrow specialization, subjects representative of the general fields of human interest must be studied. To prevent mere superficial acquaintance with a wide range of material, one subject must be chosen for special study, a definite amount of time to be devoted to it and to subjects related to it.

All subjects of the academic curriculum are divided into four main groups, as follows:

Group I. Fine Arts. Art, Dramatics, and Music.

Group II. Languages and Literatures. English, French, German, Greek, Italian, Latin, and Spanish.

Group III. Sciences. Biology, Chemistry, Home Economics, Mathematics, and Physics.

Group IV. Social Studies. Economics, Education, Government, History, Philosophy, Psychology, Religion, and Sociology.

Because of the general usefulness of such courses, each student is expected to take six hours of English composition in the freshman year, and two hours of public speaking before the close of the sophomore year. To develop an intelligent attitude towards one of the major problems of life, six hours in the history and literature of religion is required. A reading knowledge of one foreign language must be acquired by the end of the sophomore year. Those students who plan to do graduate work are urged to acquire a reading knowledge of two foreign languages. Aside from these limitations, great freedom of choice of subjects is permitted.

In addition to the requirements in the paragraph above, each student is expected, in order to lay the foundation of a broad, general educa-

REORGANIZATION OF COURSES. The 1936 catalog announced reorganization of Western courses into four groups: fine arts, languages and literatures, social sciences, and social studies. Instead of choosing majors and minors, students now selected a "field of concentration" with courses in "related fields." Seniors were required to take a comprehensive examination in their field of concentration.

Faculty Club. First presided over by Dean Helen Tappan, the faculty club represented an attempt to boost the morale of anxious professors during the Depression, which brought declining enrollment and salary reductions. Members produced a journal that provided faculty with an opportunity to present results of their research.

Bachelor of Music. Though Western had offered music instruction since its opening, the 1933 catalog announced a new bachelor of music program. Candidates pursued the four-year Western curriculum, concentrated in music, and took a fifth year of study in applied or public school music. Here, students practice the violin.

INTERPRETIVE DANCE. Western became one of the first institutions to provide instruction in modern dance when a course in interpretive dance was offered in 1924. This helped spur interest, and by 1935, a dance club was formed to sponsor annual spring recitals. Internationally renowned dancer and choreographer Martha Graham appeared in Presser Hall in 1936, generating more enthusiasm in the Western community.

CLARK MEMORIAL GATEWAY. In 1934, a gift from Grace Clark Cullen (class of 1906) made possible the construction of an impressive gateway at the north entrance to campus. Two stone pillars framed the drive that began opposite Spring Street and ran between Alumnae Hall and McKee Hall, meeting the old carriage drive in front of Peabody Hall. The Clark gate was razed after 1974, when the drive was rerouted to accommodate a new Miami University building.

Ida Montimer Windate. Professor of English Ida M. Windate taught at Western from 1915 to 1934. She received both bachelor's and master's degrees from Ohio Wesleyan, taught in Ohio and Illinois, worked at the Harvard Psychological Laboratory, and studied at the British Museum. With an endowment from former student Mary Kyle Michael (class of 1934), the Windate Writing Center in Peabody Hall was named for her in 1991.

Stancote House. Stancote was designed by Charles Cellarius and built in 1933 as a retirement home for Professor Windate. When she died in 1948, it became Western property and was used as the official residence for the dean of the college.

Westerniana Collection. At the encouragement of President Hickok, 1920 alumna Mary Helen James (later, Mrs. Martin Lord) developed a permanent collection of historical "Westerniana" when she became college librarian in 1936. This archival collection of scrapbooks, newspaper clippings, diplomas, photographs, and ephemera was publicized with library exhibits and chapel talks focusing on Western history and traditions.

Hell Week. In 1938, Western sophomores established their own orientation week to introduce freshmen to college life. Popular practices were making new students rise at dawn and requiring them to wear large name placards or, as seen here, dress in approved apparel. Rebellious freshmen could even be "tried" by the sophomores at "Hell Court." Over time, "Hell Week" dwindled to "Hell Day," and a few kinder, gentler classes experimented with "Help" Week.

Alumnae Office. The Western Alumnae Office opened in 1937 with Margaret Haviland (class of 1930, pictured here) as the first full-time executive secretary. The first alumnae council was held in October 1938. It would help plan and host alumnae functions as well as assist with development campaigns. As treasurer of the alumnae association for 15 years, Prof. Gertrude Leonard contributed greatly to reorganizing records and increasing revenue. At her initiative, Wedgwood plates with a picture of Kumler Chapel were commissioned and became best sellers.

Campus Day. The first campus day was held in April 1938, when prospective students were invited to visit the campus and see the daily operation of the college. Campus day visitors attended chapel services, sat in on classes, visited dorm rooms, enjoyed a picnic lunch, and met informally with administrators and faculty. It was a much-anticipated annual event for years.

Peabody Players. Organized in 1939, the Peabody Players produced musicals and dramas, designed and constructed scenery, created costumes, and managed their own publicity. The club was sponsored by alumna and drama professor Helen Halsey (class of 1936). Here, the players stage the 16th-century English comedy *Gammer Gurton's Needle*. They were later invited to give a repeat performance at the Cincinnati Woman's Club.

Le Cercle Francais. Organized in 1915, Le Cercle Francais gave students interested in or studying the French language an opportunity for conversation, study, and entertainment in French. By the 1930s, the study of foreign languages had become an especially important part of Western's education for music and voice students. In this 1939 photograph, Le Cercle Francais members pose on the steps of Peabody Hall.

SOCIAL SCIENCE FORUM. These forum members gather at the lodge in 1932. The club focused on experiences of Western students and alumnae involved in social work and sponsored annual debates about current economic and social problems, including the plight of the unemployed, international unrest, and militarism.

PARLIAMENT. In 1926, the government association replaced the student league. It consisted of a parliament, composed of 40 faculty and students, and a judiciary. Parliament created and approved legislation affecting Western laws and customs, while providing a forum where students and faculty could voice opinions. In this 1937 photograph, some students and faculty members of parliament meet with Dean Helen Tappan (front row, right).

Judiciary. The judiciary adjudicated violations of college regulations and included two bodies: the highest court (pictured here) and the house council. The highest court, comprised of the president, vice president, and secretary, along with two faculty representatives, decided all major cases. The house council dealt with less serious violations of house regulations and was comprised of the house presidents, the house matrons, and dormitory proctors.

Endowment Union. The student organization shown here in 1938 increased Western's endowment during the Great Depression. The club sought to protect student families while helping build endowment through student life insurance policies, with benefits payable to parents.

Six

Wartime and Aftermath
Confronting Uncertainty (1941–1953)

Mary Moore Dabney Thomson. Elected to the board of trustees in 1933, Thomson became acting president in 1941 and was inaugurated as president in 1942. Her father was Charles William Dabney, president of the University of Tennessee and University of Cincinnati, and she attended both. Married to Alexander Thomson, president of Champion Paper Co., she had five children, for which the Golden Rule Foundation named her American Mother of the Year after her nomination by the student body in 1943. During her presidency, spent entirely during war years, the curriculum was expanded to include courses in occupational training, a nursery school was opened, and summer school was initiated. She resigned in 1945 for health reasons but continued to serve on the board of trustees until 1953.

War Council. Photographed in 1942, the council was composed of students and faculty who coordinated such war activities as organizing air raid drills, inviting speakers, and providing reading materials. Students played an important part in the wartime activities of Oxford by serving as hostesses at the USO and working with local church groups and organizations at Miami University to organize blood drives for the Red Cross.

Western Defense Program. Radio was an important means of communication during World War II and for Western students in 1942. Contributing to the nationwide effort, students at Western offered community courses in defense, practical first aid, and home nursing. Students donned jeans and sang "It can happen here, fire watchers, and roof watchers" and "Messenger girls and stretcher bearers spring to their posts when the signal sounds."

HISTORY

Background of the War *3 semester hours credit*

Open to students who have completed a college course in European history or by consent of the instructor and the academic dean.

A critical survey of Europe in its world setting during the twenty-year armistice, 1919-1939. Both the international and the national developments which led to a renewal of war are studied. ***Mr. Esterquest***

WAR CURRICULUM. The "Background of War" was offered as a course in the 1943 Summer School Catalog, along with "Industrial Organization," "Specialized Radio Techniques," "Military German," and "German Literature Translation." As Western's curriculum adapted to wartime needs, it offered a combination of liberal arts courses plus basic training in occupational therapy, radio, and social welfare. Courses in Morse code and film were also added.

VICTORY GARDENS. Miriam Fatout (class of 1944), nicknamed "Miss Defense Program," perches on a piece of farm equipment in 1942. With the guidance of Prof. Rudolph Syring, a parcel of 11 acres south of the gymnasium was set aside for Victory Gardens. In a spirit reminiscent of the 1918 Farmerettes, participants were able to provide an adequate supply of vegetables for Western.

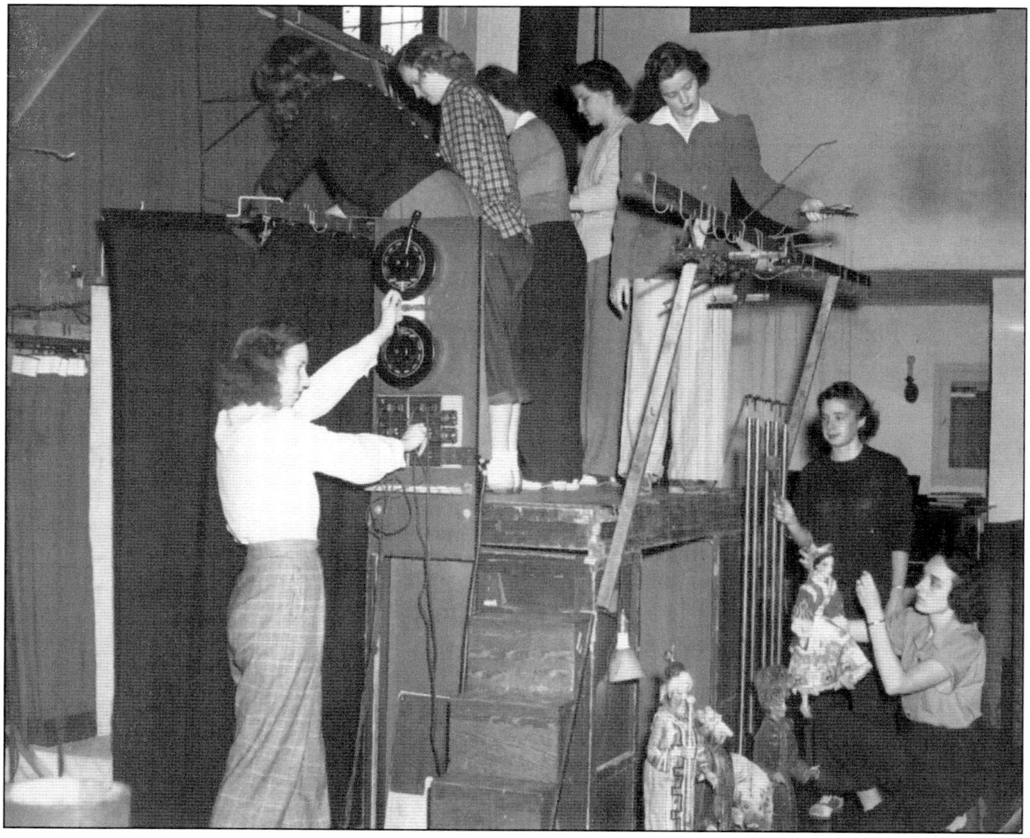

Tatterman Marionettes. Students manipulate marionettes as part of the troupe supported by William Ireland Duncan and his wife, Ruth Cliver Duncan (class of 1927), who both joined the Western faculty in 1942. They introduced courses in puppetry, acting, and stagecraft; offered performances in Presser Hall; and held national conferences on puppetry. During the war, Ruth visited government hospitals, and students performed in local high schools and in surrounding states.

Leonard Theatre. Under the direction of William Duncan, the little theater, formerly the chapel in Peabody Hall, was modernized, redecorated, and dedicated to Gertrude Leonard on April 28, 1944. Gertrude (pictured) had offered the first course in play production in 1920 and was a guiding force in the construction of the Ernst Nature Theatre in 1921.

Theater Department. A production of *Little Women* in December 1944 featured, from left to right, Betty Anne Martin, Anne Long, Vivian Hudson, Lee Cook, and Dorothy Mershon. Under the Duncans' direction, a theater department was established the following year, and a major in theater was offered. Students received instruction and experience in production, speech, and in cooperation with the physical education department, dance techniques.

Radio Station. On February 9, 1945, Western held the formal opening of its radio studio, becoming the first women's college in the country to broadcast daily over commercial airwaves. Under the direction of Duncan, students not only learned various phases of broadcasting and radio production but also completely managed and hosted their own daily show via a link to station WMOH in Middletown. Shown here on the air are, from left to right, Maxine Murray, Dorothy Mershon, Jane Winwood, Rinda Philp, and Mary Ellen Leckie.

Board of Trustees. The first woman elected to the board in 1887 was Olivia Meily Brice (class of 1866). Gathered in 1945, board members are, from left to right, (first row) Susan Wade Peabody (niece of Helen Peabody, who served after 1919 and was named honorary life trustee in 1954), Emily Jack Duncan Goldthwaite, Mary Holliday Shuler, Mary Carothers Bower (class of 1927), and Mary Moore Dabney Thomson (president); (second row) Rev. Jesse Halsey, John Molyneaux, Harry Brent Mackoy, Don W. Fitton, Claude M. Lotspeich, and William Procter Matthews.

Philip Eldon Henderson. Educated at the University of Colorado and Harvard Graduate School of Business Administration, Philip Henderson served as assistant to the president and vice president before becoming president when Thomson retired in 1945. His administration dealt with fluctuating enrollment plus administrative and financial problems but established an admissions office and oversaw the construction of Clawson Hall and Science (later, Boyd) Hall. Students remembered their popular "alphabetical teas" and buckwheat cake parties at Patterson Place long after the Hendersons left Oxford in 1951.

CENTENNIAL CAMPAIGN. Alumnae gave generously to increase faculty salaries, liquidate debt on new buildings, and increase permanent endowment in a campaign launched on October 12, 1948. This item from the *Hamilton Journal-News*, August 15, 1952, announces the campaign theme "Man's right to knowledge and his free use thereof." Campaign events included convocation, symposia, and an alumnae banquet. The campaign goal was $400,000. (Courtesy of *Journal-News*, Hamilton, Ohio.)

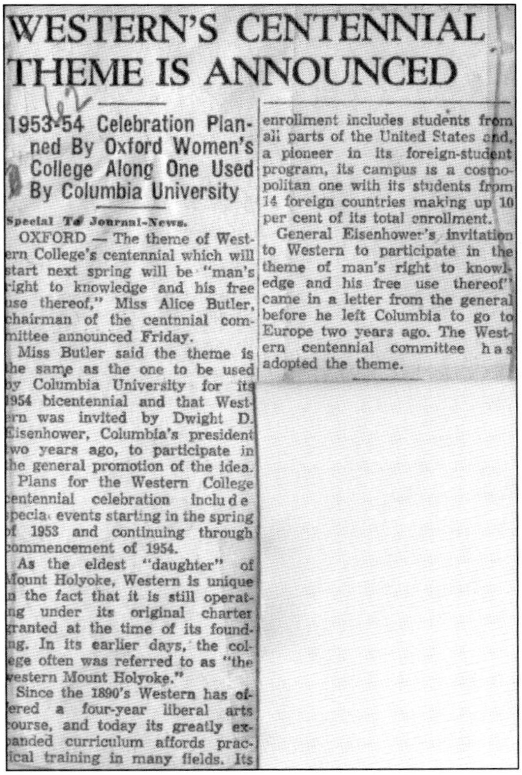

WESTERN'S CENTENNIAL THEME IS ANNOUNCED

1953-54 Celebration Planned By Oxford Women's College Along One Used By Columbia University

Special To Journal-News.

OXFORD — The theme of Western College's centennial which will start next spring will be "man's right to knowledge and his free use thereof," Miss Alice Butler, chairman of the centnnial committee announced Friday.

Miss Butler said the theme is the same as the one to be used by Columbia University for its 1954 bicentennial and that Western was invited by Dwight D. Eisenhower, Columbia's president two years ago, to participate in the general promotion of the idea.

Plans for the Western College centennial celebration include special events starting in the spring of 1953 and continuing through commencement of 1954.

As the eldest "daughter" of Mount Holyoke, Western is unique in the fact that it is still operating under its original charter granted at the time of its founding. In its earlier days, the college often was referred to as "the Western Mount Holyoke."

Since the 1890's Western has offered a four-year liberal arts course, and today its greatly expanded curriculum affords practical training in many fields. Its enrollment includes students from all parts of the United States and, a pioneer in its foreign-student program, its campus is a cosmopolitan one with its students from 14 foreign countries making up 10 per cent of its total enrollment.

General Eisenhower's invitation to Western to participate in the theme of man's right to knowledge and his free use thereof" came in a letter from the general before he left Columbia to go to Europe two years ago. The Western centennial committee has adopted the theme.

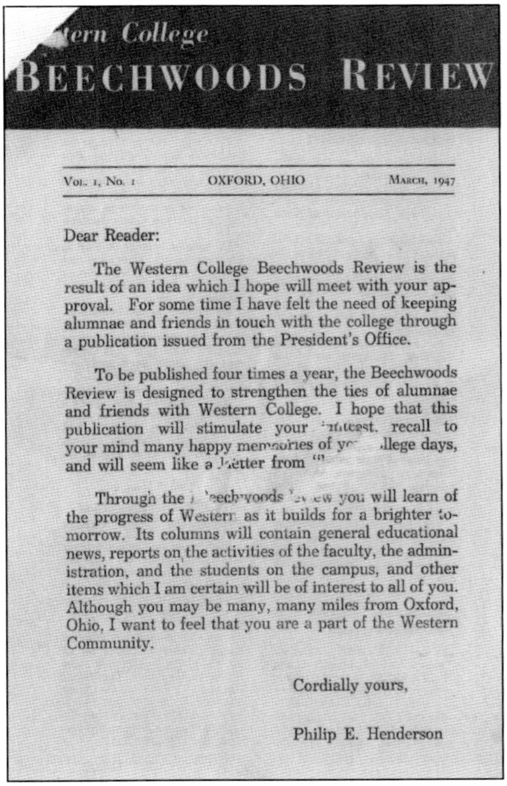

Western College

BEECHWOODS REVIEW

VOL. 1, NO. 1 OXFORD, OHIO MARCH, 1947

Dear Reader:

The Western College Beechwoods Review is the result of an idea which I hope will meet with your approval. For some time I have felt the need of keeping alumnae and friends in touch with the college through a publication issued from the President's Office.

To be published four times a year, the Beechwoods Review is designed to strengthen the ties of alumnae and friends with Western College. I hope that this publication will stimulate your interest, recall to your mind many happy memories of your college days, and will seem like a letter from [illegible]

Through the Beechwoods Review you will learn of the progress of Western as it builds for a brighter tomorrow. Its columns will contain general educational news, reports on the activities of the faculty, the administration, and the students on the campus, and other items which I am certain will be of interest to all of you. Although you may be many, many miles from Oxford, Ohio, I want to feel that you are a part of the Western Community.

Cordially yours,

Philip E. Henderson

BEECHWOODS REVIEW. This quarterly publication was created and mostly written by President Henderson to enable alumnae and other friends to keep in touch with news from the college. The paper reached a group not usually served by student publications. The first issue appeared in March 1947 and included a cover letter from President Henderson.

Science Hall. Science played an integral role in the Western curriculum, with biology classes taught as early as 1856. Students in the above photograph are working in the laboratory, included when Alumnae Hall was built in 1892. Shortly after World War II, at the urging of President Henderson, the board of trustees voted to build a science hall, pictured below. Built as a center for scientific studies, it housed classrooms, offices, laboratories, a conference room, and a greenhouse. Acknowledged as one of the finest in the Midwest, its well-equipped laboratories filled a need expressed 50 years earlier. (Bottom photograph by Jeff Sabo, Miami University.)

Boyd Hall Dedication. In 1963, Science Hall was renamed Boyd Hall. Marion Boyd Havighurst, daughter of former Western president William Waddell Boyd and wife of Miami professor Walter Havighurst, looks on at the dedication. During his tenure (1914–1931), President Boyd was responsible for the construction or donation of nine buildings, revitalizing the campus in Western's most economically successful era. Pres. Herrick B. Young stands behind the speaker.

Edith Clawson Hall. At the same time they were planning the science building, trustees began plans for an additional dormitory. Alumnae adopted it as their project, contributing generously, and the fund was greatly increased by a gift in the will of alumna Edith Clawson. The new dormitory, designed by Charles Cellarius, was named for her and dedicated on Tree Day in May 1948. (Photograph by Jeff Sabo, Miami University.)

EDITH CLAWSON. A 1900 Western graduate and native of Hamilton, Ohio, Edith Clawson earned a bachelor's degree from the University of Chicago and taught in its School of Education high school. From 1917 to 1920, she was general secretary and acting treasurer of the Hamilton Red Cross chapter. In 1933, she was the first alumna elected by alumnae to serve on the Western board of trustees and, in 1937, was made a permanent member. She died in 1944.

EDMUND H. KASE JR. President Kase presided over Western for only two years, from 1951 to 1953. Previously, he had served as associate professor of biblical literature at Wilson College and was a graduate of Princeton University and the Princeton Theological Seminary. He came to Western with many new ideas, including Western Three, a movement to secure small gifts to assist the centennial campaign. (Photograph by George R. Hoxie.)

NARKA NELSON. Dr. Nelson, a 1920 alumna and classics professor, wrote *The Western College for Women, 1853–1953*, published in 1954. Twelve years later, she agreed to add to the history, and a second edition was published in 1967. With warmth, humor, and deep affection, it records the growth of Western College and its contribution to the history of liberal arts education in the Midwest. Like many alumnae, she maintained ties to Western and donated part of her estate to the college when she died in 1974.

SENIOR HOWL. Aboard the riverboat *Delta Queen*, these students are participating in a popular Western tradition. To "howl" was to announce one's engagement. It began in the 1890s at an annual senior picnic. In later years, seniors would depart campus to the ringing of the chimes, bound for a stay of several days in an undisclosed location. Ritual and mystery were the order of the day, but enthusiasm began to decline in the late 1960s, and by the 1970s, the howl was no more.

Class Songs. Some classes were more musically inclined than others, so not all classes followed this tradition. Humorous, upbeat adaptations such as "Miss Peabody" and "We Don't Know Nothin' Yet!" were especially popular and sung by all. Betty Vandersluis, a member of the class of 1951—dubbed "the Singing Class"—adapted a beautiful contemporary melody to write the sentimental "Western Blue." (Courtesy of National.)

Class Stunts. This photograph appeared in the local newspaper in 1943, showing sophomores erecting a huge sign near Peabody Hall. "Orange is My Mother's Henhouse" was a stunt to be performed in Presser Hall. Class stunts were original productions, performed for the entire student body on special occasions. They were secretly written, usually comic, invariably included music and dance, and occasionally featured faculty participation.

Class Flags. One of Western's most cherished traditions was the creation and presentation of class flags. From the simple numerals seen here, designs evolved to include mottos and elaborate symbols in class colors. Freshmen worked all year to construct their flag in secret, with every member of the class taking one stitch. Finally, the huge flags were dramatically revealed and hung across Western Drive in front of Peabody Hall as part of the spring Tree Day ceremony. In 1956, when Tree Day merged with College Day, celebrated in October, flag raising continued to be held in May, and Flag Day was born.

Junior Garb. The custom of "junior garb" began in 1929 as juniors put on small caps in imitation of senior mortarboards, a practice proving so popular that complete ensembles in class colors were tailored for every member of the class. These were kept secret until the "big reveal," with a grand entrance en masse into Kumler Chapel or at another special program. Thereafter, all donned the garb on important occasions. Pictured here in 1958, juniors Gail Budelman (left) and Sue Marquis model their garb, a matching yellow skirt and sweater with brown monogram.

ATHLETIC ASSOCIATION. Formed in 1894, the "AA" became very active in the 1910s and 1920s, continuing the tradition of organized sports initiated under the leadership of Leila McKee. This program from the 1921–1922 season announces intramural sports and athletic activities meant to interest not only skilled athletes but the entire student body. In 1961, the athletic association became the recreation association.

ATHLETIC ASSOCIATION CABIN. A gift of alumnae and friends, the AA (later, RA) cabin was built in 1951 by Western College maintenance staff in the Beechwoods, west of the bridle path behind what is now Thomson Hall. It stood until 1974. Students did some of the carpentry themselves and used it for picnics, weekend camping, and club activities. Gail James (right), physical education instructor, and Alice Merwin (class of 1951) prepare to cross the threshold. (Photograph by Robert C. Crow.)

WESTERN FIELD DAY. Field Day became a long-standing tradition at Western, beginning in the fall of 1896. For one day, students put aside their books to participate in tennis, cricket, basketball, and track-and-field events. This 1913 photograph shows Gretchen Moeller with a winning shot put of 24 feet and 2.25 inches. She was also credited with making a basketball shot from center court.

GYMNASTICS CLASS. Gymnastics were thought to be a remedy for ailments. Here, students participate in a gymnastics class at Sawyer, with equipment hanging from the rafters. One of the first organized sports at Western, gymnastics was introduced by Miss Hattie Ege, a faculty member during 1891. It used the floor of the chapel and, later, Sawyer Gymnasium. Classes were offered in dumbbell practice, Indian drills, Swedish gymnastics, hoop drills, pole twirling, and fencing.

BASKETBALL. Invented in 1891, basketball was introduced to Western in the spring of 1895, garnering immediate popularity. Nine teams formed in the first season, with creative names such as "National Paralyzers," "Yale," "Princeton," and "Goober Grabbers." A typical uniform consisted of black bloomers and a blouse with a cardboard "W" pinned to the front.

BASEBALL NINE. The Baseball Nine from about 1895 was one of many such teams at Western, including the Tall Nine, Brownie, and Big Nine. Beginning in 1894, baseball was the most popular spring sport, and in 1895, a new diamond was built. Uniforms consisted of navy bloomers, shirts with an embroidered "W" on the chest, black stockings, and gymnasium shoes.

Golf. Only the third in the country to be built on a college campus, this golf course designed by English expert William Dunn in 1895 is enjoyed by students at the turn of the century. Golf was so popular that students would play in the winter, searching the snow with frozen fingers for their balls. In other times, the course fell into neglect. Rejuvenated in the late 1930s and again in 1953, golf declined during Western's last years.

Ice Skating. Skating at Western was never a team sport but a natural pastime during winter months, as demonstrated by students around 1900. When the pond was frozen, it was typical to see students skating before bonfires all around the pond's perimeter. Skaters were obliged to be on the lookout for the occasional open hole left after blocks of ice were cut for storage in the Ice House.

Horseback Riding. This 1934 photograph shows the campus riding club, established in October to provide both students and Oxford residents the opportunity for horseback riding. The club initiated its first autumn horse show in 1937; it became so popular that Miami students participated as well. By 1951, the club became known as the "block and bridle club."

Synchronized and Speed Swimming. After the completion of Sawyer Gymnasium, swimming became a popular activity. A swimming exhibition began in 1916, and swimming was included in the physical education requirements. Western's first intramural swim meet was held in May 1925. The Polliwogs formed a club for speed swimming, while the Dolphins specialized in synchronized swimming.

Field Hockey. This sport was first mentioned in a Western publication in 1912, and in 1924, an English hockey coach came to Western to demonstrate the game's fundamentals. This led to the blue and white all-star game, which was traditionally played on Thanksgiving Day. Though the Great Depression marked a declining interest in competitive sports, this recreational team played in 1939.

Archery. Poised to let arrows fly, these students practice archery skills on the front lawn of Clawson Hall in the 1970s. Archery was a popular intramural sport, and practice sessions could be substituted for gym credits. The archery team competed in play days at Miami and the University of Cincinnati from around 1930 to 1950 and participated in the Women's Archery Intercollegiate Telegraphic Tournament in 1937.

Bicycling. Students pose with bicycles in front of Clawson Hall in 1973. Bicycling, or "wheeling," became popular at Western around 1890, the era of the "bicycle girl." Finding enjoyment in bicycling, Pres. Leila McKee and her faculty were known to ride a track circling the athletic field. In May 1896, a bicycle club made an excursion to College Corner—a round-trip of 12 miles—and, within a year, had the largest membership of any athletic club.

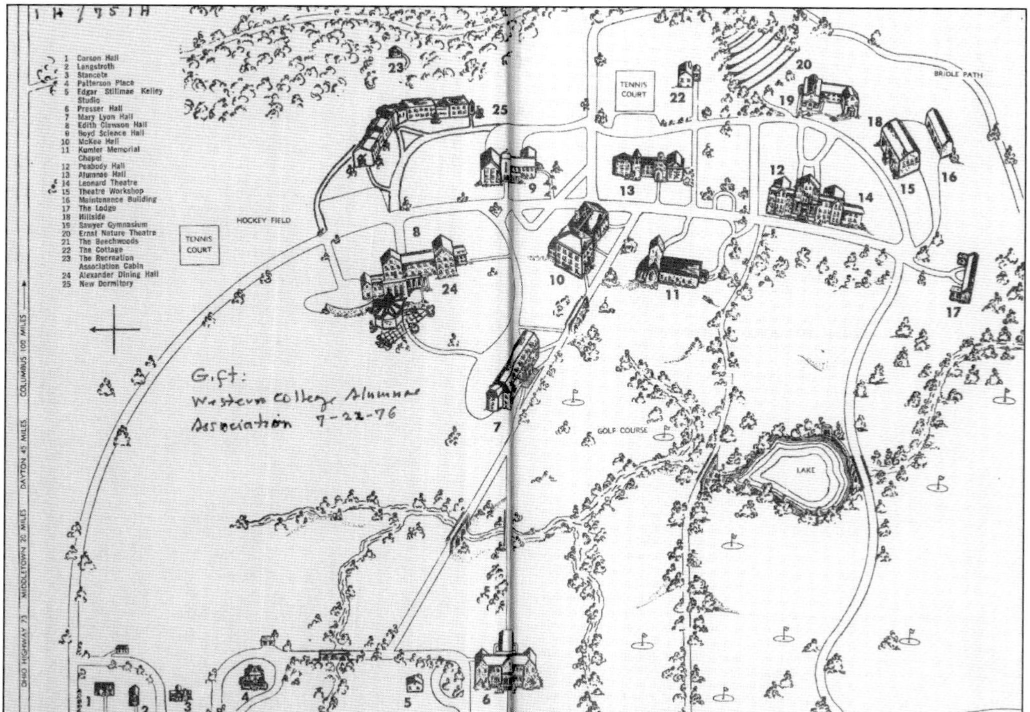

Campus Map. This map of the Western campus from 1967 shows the college grounds six years prior to Western's merger with Miami University. The hockey field, Beechwoods, Recreation Association Cabin, bridle path, and other features disappeared from the scene. Alumnae Hall would be razed by Miami. Corson House would come down to make room for a Miami building.

Seven

INTERNATIONAL FOCUS

PUTTING WESTERN ON THE GLOBAL MAP (1953–1969)

HERRICK B. YOUNG. Educated at Indiana University and Columbia University, Pres. Herrick Young served as executive secretary of the Presbyterian Board of Foreign Missions, was executive director of the International House Association, and had recently been elected to the Western board of trustees when he was asked in 1953 to become president. He officially took office on January 1, 1954, and held that position until 1969. An extensive world traveler with vast international experience, he was a perfect fit for the new intercultural plan. Under his guidance, Western became a leader in international and multicultural education. (Photograph by Blackstone Studios.)

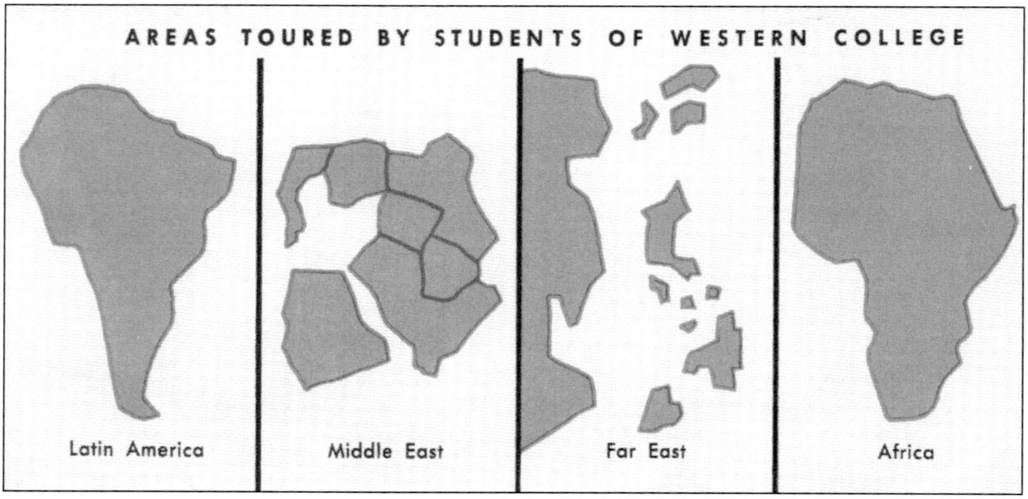

INTERCULTURAL STUDIES. A faculty plan to develop "a broad program of international education" was introduced on June 1, 1953. It included new courses, an increase in the number of students from abroad, and the appointment of international scholars as faculty. President Young further refined the plan by establishing a four-year study cycle of the "areas of special interest" shown in this illustration: Latin America, Middle East, Far East, and Africa. Following a year's intensive study of one of these areas, Western students toured the region during a summer seminar trip.

AUDIENCE WITH KING HUSSEIN. In 1960, members of the Middle East seminar, including students, faculty, administrators, and friends of the college, had an audience with King Hussein of Jordan. Prof. Gail James, who served as associate director on 11 trips, is greeted with a handshake from the king.

April Conference Focuses On Middle East

Dupree Fisher Foroughi Hulac Young

The Middle East—its history, culture, problems—will be the subject of this year's Area Conference Saturday, April 18, in Presser Hall from 9:00 a.m. to 4:30 p.m. Five noted authorities will be the speakers at the morning sessions and will lead the discussions at the afternoon workshops.

The registration fee for the conference is $1, excluding the cost of the luncheon. Further information may be obtained by writing to the College Development Office.

Speaking on "Afghanistan" will be Dr. Louis Dupree, anthropologist with the American Universities Field Staff. As a Research Associate with the American Museum of Natural History he has made two extended field trips to Afghanistan. Awarded his Ph.D. from Harvard University, Dr. Dupree has published numerous articles, reviews and monographs. The forthcoming book, **Expectant Peoples: Nationalism and Development,** will include a chapter on Afghanistan written by him.

Dr. Sydney N. Fisher, coordinator of the Graduate Institute for World Affairs at Ohio State University, will speak on "The Turkish End of the Mediterranean." A nationally recognized authority on the Middle East, Dr. Fisher is the author and editor of several books on that area. In addition to teaching at several universities in this country and abroad, he has worked with the Department of State in American relations with Turkey, the Balkans and the Near East.

Iranian Ambassador to the United States, His Excellency Mahmoud Foroughi will be the luncheon speaker. His topic will be "The History and Development of Women's Emancipation in Iran." He began his career in Teheran in 1939 with the Ministry of Foreign Affairs. He has served as Counsul General in New York, delegate to the United Nations and Ambassador to Brazil and Switzerland. He became the ambassador to the United States in April 1963.

"A Bundle of Dilemmas" is the subject of Charles R. Hulac's talk. Vice-President of the American Friends of the Middle East, he has been involved in work in the Middle East since 1946 and joined AFME in 1953, when he established the organization's first overseas program. He has worked with AFME in Iran and Jordan and has held various executive positions in the organization in this country.

Dr. T. Cuyler Young, Jr., professor in the Near Eastern Department of the University of Toronto, Canada, will discuss "Aspects of the Historical and Cultural Geography of the Near East. Dr. Young also serves as assistant curator of the Royal Ontario Museum of the University. Receiving his Ph.D. from the University of Pennsylvania, he has done extensive work in Iran with the Hasanlu Project sponsored by the University Museum of the University of Pennsylvania.

International Conferences. During this period, Western held yearly conferences, and numerous international scholars lectured in Oxford. This article announces speakers for a 1964 conference on the Middle East, featuring the Iranian ambassador to the United States, His Excellency Mahmoud Foroughi. The travel program also widened campus horizons as chaperoned students traveled to both opulent and poverty-stricken areas.

Seminar Travel. In 1966, Africa was the area of international focus for the third time, and 21 travelers accompanied President Young and his wife, Charlotte, on the last summer trip under his personal direction. Students explored historical and contemporary facets of the region via museum visits; tours of cities, national parks, and embassies; discussions with university students and professors; and music and dance concerts. (Photograph by Ojuri Commercial Photo Studio.)

Mississippi Summer Project. From June 12–27, 1964, Western's campus was the site of orientation and training for young idealistic volunteers from mostly northern states, as well as some adults, preparing to go to Mississippi to work for civil rights. This project of the Student Nonviolent Coordinating Committee (SNCC), with assistance from other groups in the Congress of Federated Organizations (COFO) and the National Council of Churches, brought international attention to Western. During the second week, word came that participants James Chaney, Michael Schwerner, and Andrew Goodman had disappeared in Mississippi while preparing to register black voters and were presumed dead. This was later confirmed. (Photograph by George R. Hoxie; courtesy of Smith Library of Regional History.)

Trustee Approval. In 1964, the Western board of trustees met to discuss the possibility of renting the college facilities to Mississippi Summer Project organizers, after their plan to meet at Berea College had been disapproved. Trustees decided to allow the sessions but stated that the civil rights cause would profit by holding this training elsewhere in 1965, if repeated.

CAMPUS BOOKSTORE. Located on the lower level of Peabody Hall, the bookstore was a popular spot for students to buy textbooks and supplies. Western souvenirs line the shelves, and students shop for bargains, such as pencils for a nickel apiece or three for a dime. In 1972, the bookstore moved to Alumnae Hall.

MUUMUU CRAZE. Students pose behind Clawson Hall, modeling a fashion fad that Western popularized. While sightseeing in Hawaii, members of the 1957 Far East seminar were captivated by these colorful, loose-fitting long dresses introduced there by missionaries. One student was the daughter of a New York dress manufacturer, who recognized their marketability and began producing muumuus in great numbers. The trend caught on at other campuses, and in 1957, *LIFE* magazine wrote a feature highlighting Western.

ALEXANDER DINING HALL. Named for alumna Bess Mason Alexander, this structure was part of a long-range development plan approved by Western trustees. Nicknamed "Alex" by students, it had a modernist character atypical for the campus when it was built in 1962. Attached to the rear of Clawson Hall, it housed a modern kitchen and a common area for cafeteria-style dining to serve a growing student population. (Photograph by George R. Hoxie.)

BESS ALEXANDER. The unrestricted gift of Bess Mason Willard Alexander (class of 1906) covered more than half the cost of the new dining hall. Originally from Bethany, Illinois, she was known to many alumnae and friends for her devotion to the college. She died in Seattle in 1960.

Thomson Hall. This 1963 residence hall was named for Mary Moore Dabney Thomson, a member of the board of trustees from 1933 to 1952 and president from 1941 to 1945. The two wings of the building are named for members of her family. (Courtesy of Miami University Publications.)

Music Faculty. A professor of music from 1947 to 1974, Eleanore Vail (receiving an award, second woman from the left) headed the music department, where she taught piano, music appreciation, and music history and performed with senior recitals. Richard Monaco (second from right) was best known as a composer of sacred music and directed the choirs. He taught at Western from 1959 until 1974. Included in the picture are Pres. Herrick Young (rear) and members of the music department.

MADRIGALS. This vocal group was very much in demand in 1966. Under the direction of Richard Monaco, the Madrigals performed a variety of music from Elizabethan to contemporary religious and secular numbers in a variety of settings—but mostly at banquets, college functions, church meetings, and civic events.

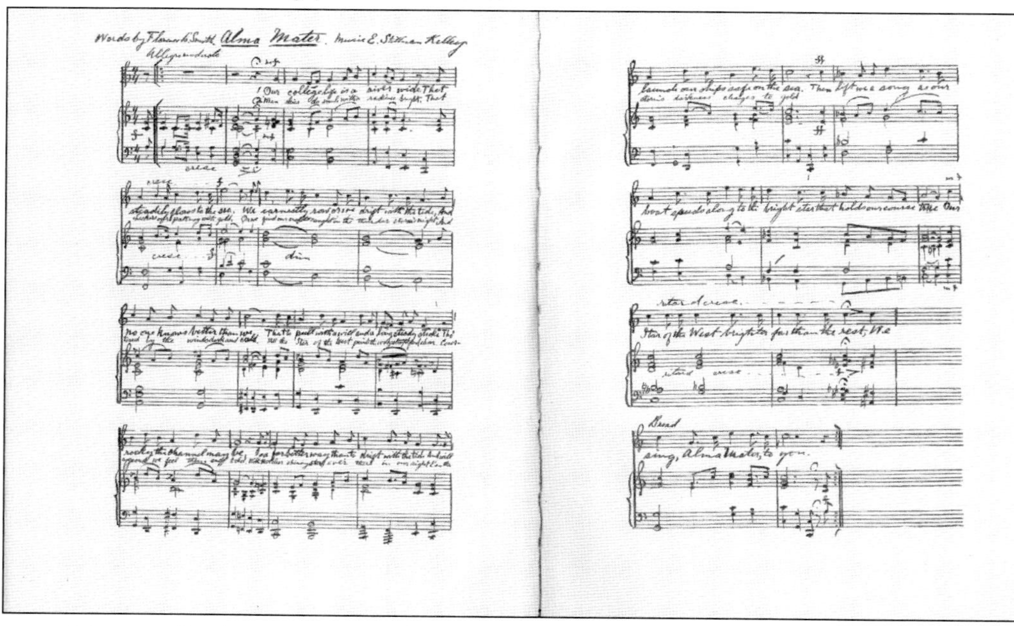

ALMA MATERS. Words to the original Western College Alma Mater were written in 1911 by Florence L. Smith (class of 1912) and set to music by Edgar Stillman Kelley. It was followed in 1961 by a new Alma Mater, with text by Narka Nelson (alumna, professor, and Western College historian) and music by Richard Monaco.

Dads' Club. Linda Barnes (class of 1961) and her father arrive at Clawson Hall during dads' club Spring Weekend. Dads' club was formed to encourage paternal participation, and the lively annual weekend became a tradition. Pleasure mixed with business as the dads elected officers and supported a variety of projects, such as increased faculty salaries, expansion of the language laboratory, new tennis courts, and renovation of the lodge and Alumnae Hall.

Powwow. The student body gathers around the Powwow bonfire in the Beechwoods on the eve of College Day in 1963. Freshmen sport their distinctive beanies, which they would wear at the freshman drill the next morning. As with most traditions, there would be changes, but class songs, a junior skit, and a dance club presentation were perennial components.

Camp Sawyer. Established in 1965 by Gail James, associate professor of physical education, this environmental day camp for young children was located primarily in the Western Lodge. In 1973, the camp instituted a program for children with above average intelligence who had learning disabilities. The camp helped children with motor skills, visual perception, and memory and included activities such as swimming, archery, tennis, dramatics, puppetry, and fishing.

Academic Procession. Crossing the bridge to Presser Hall for the 1961 commencement, President Young and faculty follow Dr. Lucy Watt (class of 1919), professor of biology from 1924 to 1963, who carries the ceremonial Western Mace. The pageantry of time-honored academic processions was much loved at Western and made part of other formal occasions in addition to graduation.

Eight

Freedom with Responsibility

Restructuring Innovatively (1969–1974)

William C. Spencer. William Spencer was assistant to the president of Columbia University and coordinator of its capital fund when named president of Western. During his tenure, men were admitted, and the name changed to the Western College. President Spencer hoped that implementing an innovative new curriculum and admitting men would overcome rising costs and scarce resources. Despite critical acclaim for its new program, Western trustees closed the college in 1974 and merged the campus with Miami University.

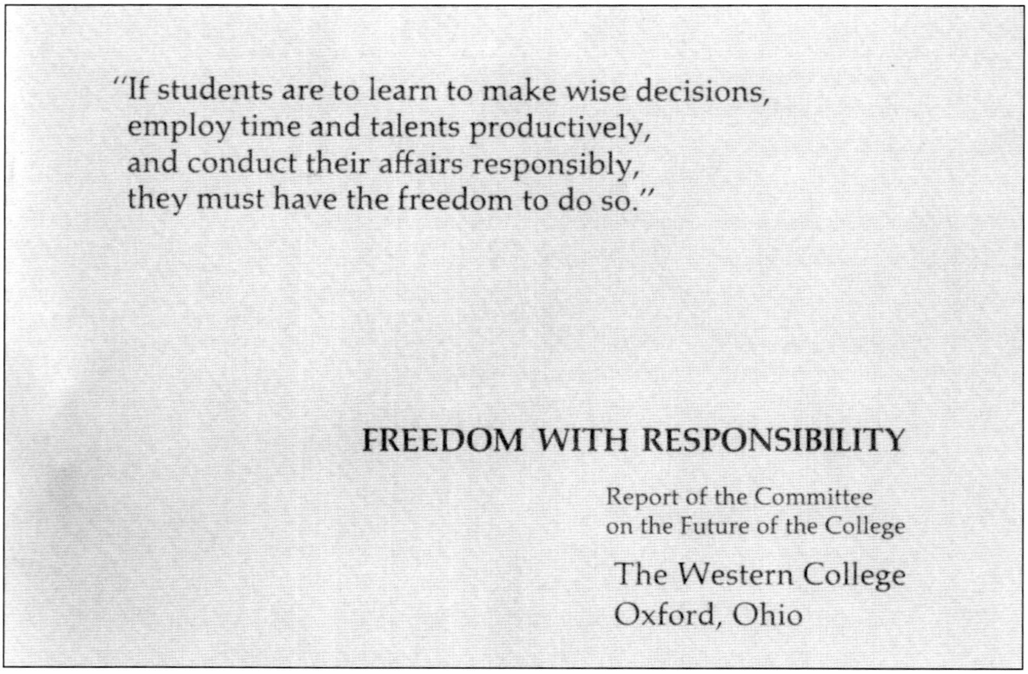
"If students are to learn to make wise decisions,
employ time and talents productively,
and conduct their affairs responsibly,
they must have the freedom to do so."

FREEDOM WITH RESPONSIBILITY

Report of the Committee
on the Future of the College

The Western College
Oxford, Ohio

FREEDOM WITH RESPONSIBILITY. In 1969, President Spencer formed the Committee on the Future of the College, comprised of trustees, alumnae, faculty, students, administrators, and emeriti. It created a program whereby faculty members designed their own learning units and students designed individualized programs with faculty consultation. Traditional letter grading was eliminated, along with conventional curricular organization. Students chose to work with faculty tutors who offered innovative options. Most projects were combined with independent studies, service commitments, field projects, and travel abroad.

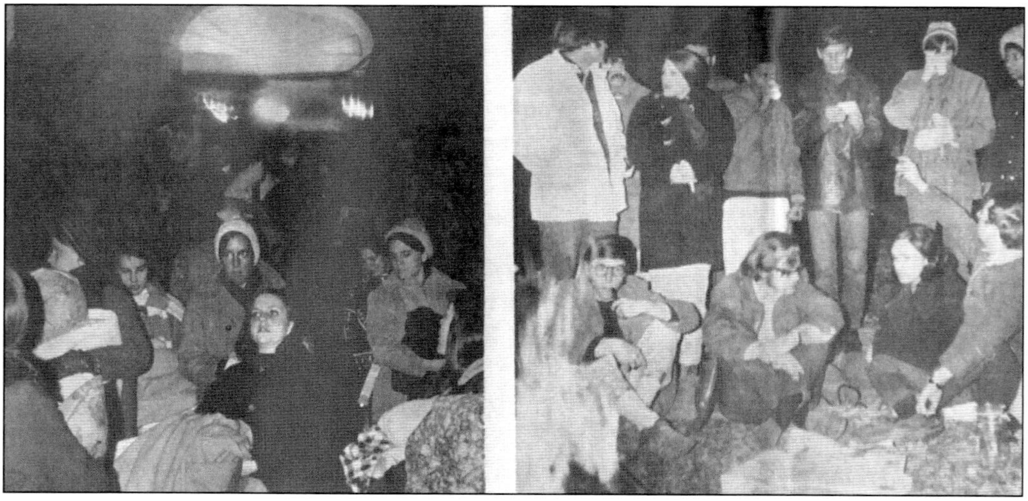

STUDENT PROTESTS. On April 14, 1969, an estimated 100 women walked out of their dormitories to protest the board of trustees' denial of their dormitory visitation proposal. With blankets and sleeping bags, they camped outside the homes of the dean and the president. Two years later, the college permitted 24-hour visitation for men. Students also held strong opinions on national issues, joining the 1967 March on the Pentagon and other Vietnam War protests and supporting refugees from the 1971 Indo-Pakistani War. (Courtesy of the *Miami Student*.)

CLASS OF 1973 FLAG. The world was in flux. The Vietnam War was under way. Students were living by rules and regulations that did not seem relevant. Military draft by lottery was to be initiated. The school was undergoing financial difficulties. A new president would take Western in new directions. The question mark, omega, and other imagery pictured here represented questions about all these matters, and perhaps more.

Introducing

Western's

New

Students

September, 1969

BABY BOOK. This so-called "Baby Book" welcomed the 156 freshmen of the class entering in 1969, harking back to seminary days when, upon arrival, Miss Peabody asked and recorded the name of each new seminary pupil in her "little book" to make the student feel "sheltered and cared for." The Baby Book included photographs and hometowns of each freshman, so the entire campus could get to know the new students. The relatively small class was a matter of concern.

College Day and Parents' Weekend. In 1969, College Day expanded into Parents' Weekend. After guest speakers were honored and the freshman class had been officially welcomed, the academic procession exited Presser Hall and applauded freshmen as they followed them out. Freshmen wore traditional white dresses, with their class ribbons presented to them on this day.

Coeducation. In September 1971, the board voted to admit men after January 1, 1972, with status equal to women as degree candidates. Previously, men took day classes but were neither full-time students nor eligible for degrees. This change was intended to increase enrollment and address financial constraint but was not quickly successful and so did not save the college.

Whatz-It-Shop. Students in 1972 browse items on sale to benefit Western. Located in the Peabody lower level, then in Alumnae Hall, this thriving business was a nonprofit consignment outlet run by roommates Susan Lantz (class of 1974) and Susan Rasman (class of 1973). It featured handcrafted prints, etchings, block-cuts, candles, artwork, and jewelry, donated by Western and Miami University students, alumnae, townspeople, professors, and staff. Students received independent research credits for business via Freedom With Responsibility.

Contemporary Chapel Service. Here, students are participating in contemporary services in Kumler Chapel with Dr. Richard Monaco leading the music. Under the auspices of the Miami-Western Cooperative Campus Ministry and the Kumler Memorial Chapel Committee, visiting clergy from various denominations, regions, and parts of the world were invited, and pews were periodically rearranged at student request. Attendance at Sunday church services was required (after 1961, "expected") for all students until 1969.

Phyllis Hoyt. A graduate of Russell Sage College and Tufts University, Phyllis Hoyt came to Western as assistant dean and head of McKee Hall in 1946 and remained until 1974. She went on to become dean of student activities, then dean and vice president of student affairs. Dean Hoyt was friend, advocate, and role model for students, faculty, and staff. In November 1964, her open letter to alumnae explaining the administration's decision to rent the campus for the orientation of students going to Mississippi, "Thoughts on the Civil Rights Orientation," appeared in the *New York Times*. In 2000, the Western College Alumnae Association, Inc., published her memoir, *Where the Peonies Bloomed.*

Hoyt Library. A new library was built in 1971 to replace the one in Alumnae Hall. Located south of Mary Lyon Hall, it was named for Dean Phyllis Hoyt as a result of students petitioning the board of trustees. Repeating a ritual from the 1890s, students hand-carried college library books to the new building. Its plaque inscription to Dean Hoyt, composed by trustees Donna Shalala (class of 1962) and Martha McKee Keehn (class of 1943) concludes, "She embodies all that has been the spirit of the Western College."

LIBRARIES. Western's original books were housed in Seminary Hall but were lost in the first fire there in 1860. Eventually, a library was built in Alumnae Hall, shown here in 1967. In 1971, with the move to Hoyt Library, the library claimed a dedicated building with more space for students, collections, research, and study.

Donavon Auble. Dr. Auble came to Western in 1954 and served the college until 1974. An associate professor and chairman of the department of psychology, he became acting dean from 1968 to 1969 and vice president for administration in 1970. Responsible for public and external affairs, he oversaw personnel functions, student recruitment, admissions, alumnae affairs, development, public relations, and publications. He chaired the Committee for the Future of the College that created Freedom With Responsibility.

Marianne Micks. Beginning at Western in 1960 as an associate professor in the department of religion, Dr. Micks chaired the department from 1962 to 1966 and was dean of the college, the principal administrative officer for academic affairs, from 1966 to 1972. Dr. Micks led the transition to the Freedom With Responsibility program.

Rosezelia Patton. Like so many Western College staff members—several of whom were recipients of *Multifaria* dedications—Rosezelia Patton was known to faculty and students alike for her positive, upbeat, and friendly manner. As registrar from 1969 to 1974, she was a constant presence on campus. A Cincinnati resident, she frequently extended invitations to students and their families to visit her home. She made a special effort to support students during final examinations.

Williard Keebler. With a Miami bachelor's degree and a master's from Harvard, "Will" Keebler started at Western in 1956 as a part-time accountant. He became business manager, then vice president of business and financial affairs. A "master juggler" who negotiated with creditors, he oversaw budgetary matters through Western's final years, including an unsuccessful attempt by trustees, alumnae, staff, faculty, and students to raise $400,000 and balance the budget in 1971. In this photograph from the *Miamian*, August 9, 1973, he is shown (at right) discussing the "affiliation and merger" agreement approved on June 15, 1973, by which Miami would assume all grounds, physical facilities, and assets in return for resolving Western's debt.

Final Commencement. From left to right, President Spencer, commencement speaker Martha McKee Keehn (class of 1943), trustee Donna Shalala (class of 1962), and trustee Stuart Fitton take part in the last official graduation. The final commencement service was held on June 8–9, 1974, when 80 undergraduates received degrees. The last undergraduate to receive a degree from Western College was Janice Robinson Wright, of Grosse Pointe, Michigan.

Spencer and Shriver. On June 21, 1973, the *Oxford Press* pictured Miami University president Phillip R. Shriver (left) and Western College president William C. Spencer at a press conference, addressing the terms of the "affiliation and merger." The presidents also announced Miami's purchase of McKee Hall prior to further developments. Implementation documents to follow stated that, after June 30, 1974, the campus would be known as "The Western College of Miami University." (Courtesy of *Oxford Press*.)

The Mature Campus. An aerial photograph made in Western's final decade shows the sweep of the campus, the length of Western Drive from Patterson Avenue (bottom) to Peabody Hall (top right). It includes the college's oldest building, Peabody, and its newest, Thomson Hall (first building on the left of the drive when moving south). With rolling hills and steep ravines, dense woods and winding creeks, and architecturally diverse buildings, this idyllic campus—crisscrossed first by footpaths, then walkways and stone bridges—was the perfect setting for a remarkable institution.

Miami University Libraries invites you to view the following online collections and websites:

Western College Memorial Archives
http://westernarchives.lib.miamioh.edu/

Western College Roundup Newspaper Collection
http://doyle.lib.muohio.edu/cdm4/westernnews/

Western College Alumnae Association
http://miamioh.edu/University_Advancement/wcaa/

Miami University Center for Digital Scholarship
http://cds.lib.miamioh.edu/services/